MW01282064

Parenting Twins

The Handbook for Containing Chaos and Preserving Memories in the First Year

Elise Moultrup Bruderly, MSW

ISBN-10: 1502414252
ISBN-13: 978-1502414250

DEDICATION

This book is dedicated to my twins, Charlotte and Owen,
who gave me the ticket to this VIP ride
in the amusement park of life.

And to my husband, Michael, my partner in love and in life.
You are the clock on which my twelve exists.

ACKNOWLEDGMENTS

A special thank you to my parents, David and Donna
Moultrup, for teaching me to be a parent my entire life. To my
extended family- my sister, my in-laws, and my extended-
sibling family- for being part of the chaos with us. And to
Michele Bickett, for being that one-in-a-million friend through
all that life has thrown us. Finally, thank you to my Aunt
Sandy, the artist in my life, for the cover design- the bow on
the entire project! The writing of this book brought back so
many memories of my first year with twins and made me,
again, appreciate how many people were involved in getting me
through. Whether it was the constant support of my family,
"strangers" from the twins group who brought me meals, and
all of the friends, with twins and without, who have been there
during various stages of my twins' lives, I "survived" because
of all of you. Thank you for sitting on the phone with me on
the bad days and celebrating the small successes on the good
days. The experiences of parenting have truly been more fun
because I was able to share them with all of you.

CONTENTS

Appendices

1 INTRODUCTION

No matter how you become pregnant with twins, no matter how far into your pregnancy you carry them, no matter how long you spend with them in the neonatal intensive care unit (NICU) or following up on medical issues, there will be a day when you will bring them home. This book is designed for that moment; and for the countless moments of joy and frustration that follow. After months of pregnancy, after weeks of worry, after hours of labor and delivery, there will be a time, surreal as it may be, that they come home. That moment you carry your babies into your home for the first time brings on an indescribable feeling. I remember taking my babies out of their car seats and laying them on pink and blue blankets on the floor. I remember sitting down on the floor with them, my mind almost blank. The world was quiet and my babies were home. It is a precious memory.

When I was pregnant, all I thought to read were books about being pregnant. There are so many of them, and there is so much new to know and understand. It did not occur to me until after my babies were here, however, that I should have spent some of those precious months with them contained in utero preparing myself to parent. It was only later that I realized how much more I needed to know and figure out. The books that I turned to- the ones to help me know what to expect and guide me from a girlfriend's perspective- were only sort of helpful. I had the issues those books focused on, sure, but I also had two babies who needed me at the same time. As I stumbled through those first days, weeks, and months with twins, I always wished I had a manual. This is the guide that would have been helpful to me.

I do not believe that there is always a right or wrong way to do things. Actually, I think you can be successful with many different parenting strategies. I do believe that the more information you have, the better a system you can implement. Whether it is for feeding or sleeping in the early months, or for discipline and interacting with the world as the kids grow, having a system can do wonders for your self esteem as a parent and for your brain when it's just too tired to figure out what to do next or how to get through a situation.

This book is designed to be a handbook- part story, part advice- to help you build your own routines and confidence. I tell my personal story at the beginning, to give you a sense of who I am and how I came to be a mother of twins. Throughout the book, topical information is woven together with my actual journal entries from the first year of life with my twins. The journal was posted on a website which I shared with my family and friends, so that they could keep up with us despite geographical distance.

This book is designed to help you keep perspective- to calm you through the difficult and trying times and to highlight and capture some of the moments that make it all worthwhile. Welcome to twin parenting.

2 PARENTING TWINS

When I was pregnant, everyone told me that I had no idea what I was getting into. I was certain that this was true, but I also felt relatively confident that I could handle whatever it was that would come up. I had a lot of experience with children when I was young. I spent my childhood years playing with any baby I could find, my teenage years babysitting, and my early adult years knowing that above all else in life, I wanted to have a family.

It was this confidence in my ability to handle whatever happened once the baby was here that allowed me to focus all of my anxiety on being pregnant. This anxiety, a completely normal amount, I'm sure, took on a whole new cast at the discovery that I was having twins. Then my anxiety was exponentially multiplied (no pun intended) as the medical community switched on their anxiety button. I had to switch doctors, moving my care to the high risk OB department. I found that my pregnancy would have greater oversight and be more frequently monitored. This again allowed me to focus all of my energy on the pregnancy. Now, I'm not claiming that this was an inappropriate amount of medical care, as I am well aware of the vast number of issues that mom and babies face together. As both my babies were breech, I am convinced that without modern medicine it is unlikely that all three of us would have made it through the birth process unscathed. Had I known then, however, what I know now, I would have spent much more of this pre-children time learning about parenting, particularly the challenges of parenting multiples!

I'm not quite sure where regular parenting ends and parenting twins begins. As my twins are my first children, my experience is that of a first time parent, except that I'm doing it twice, and first, at the same time. I have said on dozens of difficult days that I'm doing this "wrong, twice, for the first and last time!" I am, of course, referring to the fact that I'm not feeling competent, that two children are suffering the results of that incompetence, that I've never done it before, and that I'm not planning on doing it again with any more children! I cannot say, exactly, how much would be different and how much would remain the same if I were only caring for one child. I will admit, though, that I have moments, generally everyday, where I am painfully aware of the challenges of having two at the same age and developmental stage.

How much less time might it take to get from point A to point B if you didn't have to wrestle two children into full winter gear (with the first victim of your dressing undressing while you are dressing victim two), and into car seats (while each child takes their turn screaming and arching their back in order to avoid the five-point harness, all the while the second child to be seated is behind the house door screaming, lest you forget they want to come too)? How different would a trip to the store be- you might actually feel like you could let your child walk and explore the world rather than feeling that both children need to be buckled securely into a stroller? And, would I feel less torn and less guilty about not having enough time, energy, patience, and arms to give my children what they are asking for at a given time?

These questions are meant to show a range of levels on which parenting twins is challenging. While parents of multiple children born at different times likely face similar issues in all of these arenas, feeling that your babies have competed, or at the very least had to compromise and share, your womb, attention, and love from the very beginning sets these issues in a different context. Even the bonding that happens during pregnancy, for example, has to be shared between the babies. Many books about twins discuss this in terms of thinking about the babies as a "unit." They talk about falling in love with the unit and having it take time as a parent, after the babies are born, to separate the babies in your own mind. All of this is happening, of course, on an emotional level. You know you are having two babies, you come up with names for both of them, you aspire to guess personality characteristics based on their activity level and the time of day they preferred to hold Olympic events in the womb. But, as you don't really know which baby is doing what (and studies confirm that even mothers are often wrong when guessing which baby is doing one thing or another in utero), you cannot bond in the way that the mother of a singleton bonds with her baby- no matter how many other children that mother is caring for at the time of her pregnancy.

Parenting twins, then, requires an additional effort that is difficult to conceptualize in the abstract, let alone with words on paper. It requires extra energy to get through the day, extra patience for each child who needs to try a forbidden behavior, extra vigilance in attending to the escapades of each child at the same time, an ability to anticipate the roadblocks to goals-whether that be getting through an airport or a meal, and extra internal strength to know that you are doing the best that you can do at any given time and to be okay with that.

Despite my determination to get out of this mode of functioning the truth is that it is very difficult. My day would revolve around any activities we had to do at particular times. I would then add in the ones that must get done regardless of the day's schedule (namely, eating and diaper changes). After this, I would add in activities that are required for the day to go as well as possible (namely, naps). Finally, I would then plan to get as much done in the rest of that time as humanly possible (generally this included only dressing all of us, preparing meals, and supervising play and destruction). While I will admit to ongoing frustration about feeling like I accomplished nothing everyday, I also hated to think that all we were doing sometimes was surviving. The honest truth, though, is that at various stages in your babies lives, it will really be all you have time for.

Of course we did have fun- the term survival is not meant as a negative, but merely a descriptor for the amount of "extra" my husband and I had in our lives. We watched two television shows every week, and found ourselves feeling an extra bit of freedom when one went on hiatus. We had to call the car dealership every so often to figure out how long it had been since we had had the oil changed- one time we found that it had been nine months. We no longer went to the mall to browse, we went to get the kids out of the house in the winter and let them run around at the play area. I would cut my husband's hair at nine o'clock at night when the salons were closed for the day. I would get my own hair cut occasionally, when the cards lined up and someone was around to watch the kids. We would squeeze as many of our chores as possible (bill paying, cleaning, and laundry) into the times that the kids were sleeping in order for us to be available to them when they were awake.

As much as I wanted to find all the answers to how to parent twins in books, I never did. For one thing, reading did not make the priority list as often as I would have liked it to. I did find that I could make time for it when something with the babies was going so wrong that I just had to figure out what to do! I have a very strong memory of pouring over my "sleep book" when the babies were about four months old. I needed sleep so badly that somehow I found time to read and reread that book throughout the day, everyday, until I had a plan. Further, the books that I had access to were not that helpful to me. I believe that there is a fine line between "scaring" and "preparing" for parenting twins. This handbook seeks to walk that line, sometimes wobbling in one direction or the other a tad bit more.

What are the most important things to know about parenting twins? Some of them may seem completely obvious, but you may find that in the "heat of the moment" it is always good to have a reminder about such things.

1) It is much easier to parent well when you are well-rested and well-fed. Because most of the time this will not be your normal state, you must keep that in mind and give yourself some extra time to chill out before responding to a situation.

2) "Help" is great, but sometimes it is not possible to find or get. You can manage with as much or as little "help" as is available to you. You can make things work.

3) The number one thing that you can do to increase your likelihood of "succeeding" is to lower your expectations. This is not a "giving up," but instead a reorganization of priorities- essential, I believe, to enjoying the twin-parenting experience.

Once upon a time ago I sat at my kitchen table writing out my life plans with one of my then best-friends on those little square colored pieces of paper that come in little plastic holders for telephone messages. At the time my life plans fit perfectly, if not on one of those squares, at least on 3 of them. My parents still have that kitchen table, but those slips of paper are lost to the years. I can only hope that someday I run across them again. Those seem like the kind of thing that I should have kept. But, then again, maybe I thought that it was so easy, so clear, and so straightforward that there was no need to reference it again. It probably went something like this: graduate from high school, go to college somewhere great, meet the man I would marry, fall madly in love and get married, have two kids, buy a house somewhere in there, and live happily ever after.

I always did like fairy tales and I saw no reason why my life couldn't be one of them. I have always felt so fortunate to have grown up in a way where my life could possibly fall in line with a fairy tale and I am so grateful to my parents for letting me dream that all things were possible. I have grown to realize, though, that reality may not always follow the straightest of lines to that happy ending. The only thing easy about parenting is falling in love with your babies. You don't get to choose what you experience as a parent nor do you get to assure the life path of your children. What you do get to choose, however, is how you respond to what life throws you. It is how you handle what comes that will affect your experience and will affect your children. Knowing what you want is only part of the battle. Keeping your head when things don't go according to plan is the key to success.

Twin parenting is an adventure, no matter how you get here. Some families have been through fertility treatments and are hopeful to fill their family, others adopt twins into their lives, and still others are surprised by an unexpectedly doubled pregnancy. Parenting twins is not something I ever expected and parts of it will never be considered fun in my eyes. I have never been a person who loves "having twins." I love my children dearly, don't get me wrong, but the "twin experience" is not something I ever considered as a goal. It has always caught me off guard when strangers passing by would tell me that they "always wanted twins." The adventure in parenting, though, is present no matter what your family structure. Parenting twins is like a VIP ride in the amusement park of life.

3 JOURNAL: SEPT 10TH

Saturday, September 10th

Well, we're at 34 weeks and basically 4 days (in a few hours). Final push, that's for sure. (No pun intended) :)

It's been a rather difficult week. I developed an extremely annoying complication "Polymorphic Eruption of Pregnancy" (PEP). Essentially, by mid-week I severely itched all over my entire body- everywhere from toes to stomach to shoulder blades. After trying everything in the book for some relief and getting nice welts all over from itching, I eventually needed to take some oral steroids. I have to say, these haven't worked as well as I hoped and it's taken 3 days to even moderately reduce the itching. I'm on a short course of the steroids, so we're hoping things don't start to get worse again, as I'm already taking a tapered/lowered dose.

But, the end is getting close. As the babies have stayed breech, and we're fairly sure there's no room for them to turn, we have a c-section scheduled for September 28th. That would put me at 37 weeks exactly. Now, I could still go into labor before that (and I'm hoping that I do) :) and if that happens and the babies are still breech I will have a c-section then. But, one way or the other, we're in the final days.

And, as delivery is the only "cure" for PEP, I am most especially anxious. :)

But, besides all the annoyance of these final days of pregnancy, we're mostly just excited to meet our babies!

4 MY STORY

My story begins in February of 2005 when I was several days into a much needed vacation with my husband in Florida. My job as a social worker had been hectic and exhausting the several weeks before we left, and my husband's work as a medical resident was at least as draining. We were off to Florida to visit family and have some fun on our own. I left town feeling wiped out and looking forward to some recuperation time. Well, I never did start feeling better, and about 5 days or so into the trip, I found out I was pregnant. Within hours of this discovery, all of the stereotypical symptoms came on- full force. I remember literally crying on the floor of the hotel bathroom after vomiting because I felt so bad. Once I found out I was pregnant, I could look back a week or two and realize that I had, in fact, had some symptoms- fatigue and nausea- the week or so before. At this point I was about 6 weeks along and all of the joy and anxiety (likely more than most people, as my husband saw his share of obstetrical issues in family medicine) that could be possible at a time like this were present.

My story probably proceeds rather commonly at this point. I saw the doctor first around 10 or 12 weeks. I will admit to having anxiety about making sure that I really was pregnant when I went into that first appointment. I did find it strange that no one "retested" me- accepting my word that a drug store test told me I was pregnant. At the time, though, I was also well aware of the fact that if I wasn't pregnant, I was really very sick! On this first visit any absurd worry I had quickly left when we heard a tiny heartbeat. I had no idea that this would be possible so early- before I even looked pregnant- and I remember feeling so much emotion that I did not even know how to express it. I remember my heart feeling very full, and I remember looking over at my husband, really just in wonderment. I think that I was dealing primarily with the amazement of hearing a heartbeat that wasn't mine- coming from my abdomen- and then thinking about the fact that that was a baby's heartbeat. It was only after that part of the appointment was finished, and after the doctor left the room for a minute that I think the full weight of this event hit me- this was *our* baby, it was really there. I didn't need to have a first trimester ultrasound because my dates were all known. Little did we know that this would come back to haunt us!

And so my pregnancy proceeded onward. I learned to deal with the insane amount of "all day" sickness that I was having. I had the timing down to a science. I knew what time I had to get up in the morning in order to eat, so that I could shower before needing to throw up everything that I ate, so that I could get to the bus on-time, so that I could get to work and into the building before I needed to throw-up again. I will say that depending on how long the bus took, sometimes I had to get to the nearest bathroom inside the door, and other times I could make it to my office, take my coat off, and turn on my pager before racing down the hallway to the bathroom. Some days were worse than others- I often had to keep my office door closed in order to hold out as many of the morning breakfast smells as possible wafting from co-workers desks. The smell of fried food really made me ill, so I had to avoid the cafeteria hallways as much as possible as I worked through the day. If I did have to pass them, I certainly couldn't breath through my nose. Even now, the smell of fried food triggers a sensory memory for me of those pregnant days.

This was my first pregnancy, so I really didn't know what to expect. I planned to wait the customary 12 weeks before telling anyone that I was pregnant. And, seeing as how I didn't find out until I was already technically 6 weeks along, I didn't see that that would be too much of a challenge. Well, interestingly enough, by 12 weeks I was having some serious trouble fitting into my regular clothes already. When I asked friends when they switched over to maternity clothes, I told by many friends that it was closer to 20 weeks for them. I felt big; and I didn't know why- after all, I hadn't been pregnant before. Well, this was my first clue that something was different with this pregnancy, though I really didn't know it. I was having to move into maternity clothes before I had even had a chance to tell many of my friends and co-workers that I was pregnant.

I specifically brought this up to my doctor during my 16 week appointment. I remember saying "I feel big" and joking that I "just wanted to make sure it wasn't twins or anything!" Now, I will tell you that under no uncertain terms did I ever imagine or believe that I was having twins, even making that joke, and even with the idea that I was feeling big. My doctor did humor me, though, and did look all over for more than one heartbeat, but we again only heard one. It was during this visit that I had some blood drawn for some screening tests. I know many people choose not to have these tests done, but we were constantly balancing the fact that my husband had always been on the physician end of this process, and he felt more comfortable knowing that we had all of the information available about how the baby was doing.

The results from the blood tests came back several days later. My husband received the news first, and then he told me. He would later tell me that it was the hardest thing he's ever had to do. He had to tell me that the results told us that our baby had an exceptionally high risk for spina bifida. Now, we knew this was a screening test, and that the results just indicated a need for further tests. However, when you are told that you have a 1:67 chance that your baby has a terrible disease, and, you are already dealing with pregnancy hormones, the emotion is overwhelming. As it happened, we received these results just before Mother's Day- and I will say that it was absolutely the worst Mother's Day that I hope I ever have. I felt disconnected from my baby, wondering if it was even going to be viable. I know that it was a self-preservation mechanism- an attempt for my mind to distance itself from what could be an extremely painful discovery- that my baby had a problem.

It was the next Thursday that we were finally able to get in for an ultrasound, a full five days after receiving the news of a possible problem. I remember those days clearly, and can easily bring to mind the feeling of those tears that sat just behind my eyelids as I anticipated the worst. We knew the results of the blood test, and, though we knew the test could be wrong for multiple reasons (including if you are, in fact, having multiples) I was also sure those reasons did not apply to me. I decided, in advance, that I did not want to look at the ultrasound during the process. If something was wrong, I did not want to have those pictures in my mind to be remembered forever. My husband honored my decision and supported me by not looking at the screen either. We asked the ultrasound technician to please not tell us anything, that we would wait to hear from our doctor. Well, the ultrasound technician knew instantly, and, in fact, asked us again, right after she started, if we were sure that we did not want to know anything. She knew that we were having twins and we thought "she just slapped the probe on me, how could she have anything to tell us that would change my mind?" It was a very long ultrasound- again, I had never had one, but it just felt like it was longer than it should be. And, she came back and had to get more pictures after it was over. At the end, the technician printed out pictures for us, and put them in an envelope for us to take home in case we wanted to change our minds later and look at them- something for which I will be eternally grateful.

In case you haven't followed, my blood test results were skewed because I had two fetuses. Luckily, both babies looked good on ultrasound. My husband again received these results before me and found me at my office the same day to let me know since he was also working in the hospital that month. I was on the phone when he came in, and I remember being in no hurry to get off the phone. I knew from the look on his face that he had news, and as much as I wanted to hear it, I was also terribly afraid. As long as I stayed on that phone call, nothing had changed- nothing was better, but nothing was worse. When I did finally, hang up the phone and prepare myself for the news, he first told me that the baby was okay. He then proceeded to say that the reason the blood test results were wrong was because there were two babies. Luckily I was alone in the office at the time he told me because I literally freaked out. I panicked. I had to lay down on the floor I was so overwhelmed with emotion. I went from worrying I was losing one baby to panicking about having to carry, give birth to, and then care for and raise two babies!

In one moment I went from a healthy, young mother with an uncomplicated pregnancy to a high-risk ob patient. It would mean changing doctors half-way through the pregnancy and new worries about complications and preterm labor. It would go on to change literally everything that I had hoped for in my pregnancy. When I thought I was having one baby I wanted to be surprised by the sex of the baby. When I found out I was having two, I decided that was enough surprises for me and that night we looked at the record. I was 17 and a half weeks pregnant with boy/girl twins.

We found out about the twins just before they really made their presence known physically. By 20 weeks I was measuring a month ahead of schedule- for a singleton pregnancy at 24 weeks. Shortly after this appointment, I believe it was at my first high risk appointment at 22 weeks, they stopped measuring me because I had surpassed the measurements for a full-term singleton. Also at 20 weeks I began having contractions, which I would learn to control somewhat by drinking insane amounts of water and spending a good portion of my non-working time laying on my left side. When I first went to the High Risk OB Clinic they recommended that I purchase a specific book about multiple pregnancies and read it immediately. I complied, and it completely inflated my anxiety. I specifically remember, though, its recommendation to reduce work hours or stop working completely by 26 weeks. At the time I read this, my first reaction was panic because that was literally just a few weeks away. My second reaction, though, was to prove it wrong. I thought I could do continue to do everything I was doing before. Well, this was not, in fact, the case. By 26 weeks I was exhausted, and not keeping up well with life. My husband accompanied me to my appointment so that he could be sure to communicate how I was doing to the doctor. I negotiated to reduce my work-hours by half, rather than to be taken off completely as was recommended. Looking back, and to help others who might find themselves at this crossroads themselves, I will say that I wish I would have just gone off completely. Who knows what difference it would have made in the end, but I now have a different view on my responsibilities as a mother. I wanted so badly to be able to do it all- to keep up with my responsibilities at work while pregnant. I better understand, now, that time moves quickly, and some opportunities you won't ever have again. Caring for your babies prior to birth is just as important as after delivery. When I cut back to half-time, I spent the rest of the day sleeping and drinking water while laying on my left side trying to minimize contractions. By this point in the pregnancy I had moved from small to large and extra-large maternity clothes, as I had grown out of all of the clothes that I expected to fit for my entire pregnancy.

As "high risk" pregnancies go, I fared fairly well. I avoided "strict" bed rest, though, for all practical purposes by the end of my pregnancy I had very little energy and ability to go anywhere. We lived in a third floor, walk-up apartment, so just getting up and down the stairs to our home was a huge task. Just shy of 34 weeks I developed Polymorphic Eruption of Pregnancy (PEPs). It caused extreme and absurd itching- the likes of which it is impossible to describe if you haven't experienced it yourself. I tried every trick in the book- from oatmeal and baking soda baths to lotion- to try to get the condition under control. As much as I wanted to avoid medication I eventually had to resort to oral steroids because the symptoms were so bad- I wanted to tear my skin off as I couldn't stand being in it. I ended up taking steroids for 3 or 4 days (without much relief) before I spontaneously went into preterm labor. Delivery is really the only "cure" for this condition, and it is true that the symptoms from the PEPs were gone just hours after delivery!

It was September, football season, and a Saturday at that. I remember being home, watching football with my husband that day. Some friends of ours called to see if we wanted to play ultimate frisbee with them in the evening. I remember telling my husband that I wasn't feeling good, but that he could go play. He didn't, he stayed home with me and we laid low for the rest of the evening. I remember that I was busy cooking extra food to freeze, and I updated the website I was using to keep our family posted on the pregnancy. I went to bed around 10pm while my husband stayed up to finish watching some football games and work on the computer.

It was around midnight when I woke up, feeling weird. I was walking out of our bedroom as my husband was walking in. I remember telling him that I wasn't sure he was going to get to go to bed that night. I wasn't sure what contractions were really like- I'd been having them since 20 weeks, but I didn't know how to distinguish what was a labor contraction, or not. The sensations I was feeling were like contractions, but they never "let up" the way they did in the movies. I called the hospital and after an hour or two of laying down, drinking water, and checking in by phone, they told me to come in. About a half hour after arriving at the hospital a nurse came in to move me to my room. I was being admitted for preterm labor. Apparently my contractions were very long and new ones were starting before the previous one let up, which is why they didn't feel like they looked in the movies!

As my babies were breech, my options were limited. After trying to stop labor for about eight hours we decided it was time to deliver. Most important to me was doing this before it was an emergency and before medical decisions needed to be made quickly. The cesarian section experience was not fabulous for me. Once the babies were out and in the hands of their own medical teams I remember being told that it would be about a half hour more before I was "done." I was, at the time, shaking uncontrollably. I later found out that this was a common part of labor and delivery (whether the babies are born vaginally or by c-section). At the time, though, I think I knew my "job" was done. I was no longer in charge of the babies. They had been born, my job for the last 34 weeks and 4 days was over. And, with that thought and the uncontrollable shaking, I lost myself to the anxiety of the situation. I had to be medicated to calm down so that I could be sewn up. I remember moments from that time-hallucinations I had from the medication, phrases that the doctors said to me, and times with my husband and nurse. It took me several hours to come out of the mental mess I was in at that time.

After delivery my nurse and husband helped me pump for the first time. Apparently your body is poised to nurse after delivery and whatever precious drops of colostrum you can pump out is good for the babies. While I was recovering from the various medications I had been given during the c-section, my husband ran back and forth between me and our babies (who were initially bedded in separate rooms in the Neonatal Intensive Care Unit). He would bring our camera back and forth with him and snap pictures so that I could see the babies I had yet to see in person. About four hours after they were born, I was able to be wheeled on a stretcher to see my babies for the very first time. They were covered in leads (lines to monitors), were swaddled with blankets, and had little hats on. It was then that we officially named them.

5 JOURNAL: SEPT 17TH & 22ND

Saturday, September 17th

Well, little did we know how prophetic that last journal entry was. Essentially, I finished writing this, decided I was tired, and went to bed around 10pm. Mike stayed up to watch football...around midnight I woke up feeling "weird" not quite sure what was going on, but knew something was "different." So, as Mike was walking in to go to sleep, I was walking out to let him know he might not get to! I felt like I was contracting, but couldn't really tell how long they were- they never seemed to let up! To make a long story short, after being in touch with the doctors a few times, we ended up at the hospital at 3am. I was monitored for about 30-45 minutes before I it was determined that I was, in fact, in pre-term labor and being admitted. We spent the next 6 hours trying to get my contractions to stop without luck. And, since it wasn't overly early, they don't use specific medications to stop labor. The twins were both still breech, so we knew we had to be making decisions about a c-section...

I'll spare you the details of the next 9 hours, but essentially, I'm not a fan of c-sections... I got to see the babies for the first time about 4 hours after they were born. The babies went to the neonatal intensive care unit (NICU) right away. Mike took the digital camera and took a few pictures so that I could see them, but I wasn't in great shape right after the c-section.

I got wheeled down to the NICU on a stretcher and got to hold both babies briefly before being taken to another room.

Over the next few days, the babies resolved their respiratory issues and gradually weaned off of the oxygen they were on. Their little personalities coming out right away. Charlotte tolerated the oxygen for a little while, then a few days in decided she had had it and took her own oxygen off. The nurses decided to see how she did without it, and she's been much happier ever since. Owen took an extra day to get his off.

Overall they are doing well. While they did have good birth weights, they are still just developmentally a little over 35 weeks. So their "suck-swallow-breathe" coordination is not that good. This is important because they need this to eat. :) So, they've been getting tube-feedings through a tube in their nose. We're working with them on both breast-feeding and bottle feeding (while our goal is breast-feeding, we're willing to do anything to get them out of the hospital and supposedly they'll be better at transitioning between the two than full-term babies). The biggest obstacle to all of this is their fatigue. Pretty much everything wears them out. While it kills us to not hold them all the time that we're with them, we're supposed to let them be if they're sleeping/resting in order to let them have strength for other times. It's been really hard to coordinate this so that we can practice breast and bottle feedings at times when they're awake.

They are, through all of this, incredibly cute. Just yesterday they were doing well enough to be "co-bedded." They now sleep in the same crib and are swaddled together. There is some research that shows that multiples do better in this type of situation in the NICU. They can regulate their breathing, temperatures, etc better than they would individually. They are very funny to watch all bundled together. It is clear now why I sometimes felt like there were major motion pictures being filmed in my stomach!

Here are some cute things we've noticed. Charlotte gets the hiccups a lot, they don't seem to bother her, which is good cause they don't go away very quickly. When she is awake, her little eyes look all over- darting back and forth just taking in everything. Sometimes it seems like she reacts when Owen cries, but we're not sure. Owen makes all kinds of funny faces and has a pouty lip already. He, also, has some very alert times and doesn't like to cave into sleep after eating. They both swat at each other now that they're sleeping together but they're both very good, and cute, and we love them very much.

It is SO hard to leave them to come home at the end of the night. We hope to get them home soon, but realistically understand that it'll likely be at least another week. The doctors are promising nothing.

Thursday, September 22nd

Well, good news for the day- Charlotte and Owen took all of their feedings overnight by bottle- no tube feeds. If they can keep this up and show that they're continuing to gain weight, we may be able to take them home this weekend. I've got every limb crossed that we don't have any setbacks. We can already see how tired they are having to spend their energy eating all day. But, they're being troopers and we keep explaining to them that this will allow them to come home with us which we assure them will make all of us happier.

The feeding issue is going to continue to be a little tricky- we'll have to take them into the doctor's office for frequent weight checks to make sure they're gaining weight. They're still so little that a minor weight loss is much more of a big deal than if they were full term. They're still about 4 weeks away from their 40 week due date and as we understand it, they will start doing much better with energy and feeding around that time.

The staff in the NICU call the 34/35 weekers (like our babies born at 34.5 weeks) the "great pretenders." For the most part they look like full term babies and we expect them to act that way, but developmentally they're just not ready yet.

So, we're still trying to limit the amount of stimulation they receive and let them rest in between feedings. Not so easy for excited parents who don't get to spend enough time with them anyways!!! It takes a lot of self-talk to put them down in their crib at the end of a feeding... but, the end of the hospital stay is approaching and we're learning a level of patience that we never thought we'd need.

They continue to make us laugh everyday- sometimes it's the little half-smile Charlotte gives as she falls asleep, other times it's the one-eyed "pirate" look Owen has as he fights drifting off to sleep. Many times it's at ourselves as we do a ridiculous job trying to change their diapers around all of the leads and monitors on the babies. Who knew diaper changing could get easier once you get them home!

We love them more and more everyday.

6 HOW PARENTING TWINS IS DIFFERENT

After I recovered from the shock of the news that I was pregnant with two little babies I settled into a generalized anxiety about the whole ordeal. And, as with any good extra amount of anxiety- you need to send it somewhere. For me, I channeled all of that anxiety and worry into choosing the right stroller. It might seem silly to some and it certainly baffled my husband. Looking back I can smile, but I also know that this was my way of exerting control over a completely uncontrollable situation. Now the story becomes even more amusing when I say that quite a bit has changed in the availability of "twin gear" since my babies were born (not even that long ago). But the range of products, the number of styles and options, and the price points are, indeed, significantly expanded now from what I had to choose from. I say this because to "choose" a stroller was not even, frankly, that big of a deal. Nonetheless, I did my research; I read online reviews, I looked at manufacturer websites, I came up with my list of desired options, I figured out what fabric pattern fit my personality. Long story short, I was convinced that if I had the right stroller, everything would be okay.

So, I did find that perfect stroller. It was perfect for me. And, perhaps because I was so convinced that it was perfect for me from the beginning, I never did covet another- as many of my friends did. Sure, it took some finagling to find the exact stroller I wanted, and sure I did end up having to purchase it from another state. Luckily, as we have family out-of-state, it was just a little bit out of the way to pick it up on their way to visit us. Now the most amusing part of all of this, I suppose, is that the double stroller and matching car seats ended up residing in the car. Our third floor, walk-up apartment was definitely not the place to store, what my father affectionately named, the "Lunar Lander."

This is a simple story which highlights the kinds of "differences" that most people think about when it comes to parenting multiples. To the casual observer, the "big" decisions parents of multiples need to make are ones like "will you dress them alike" or, as they get older, "will you keep them together in school or put them in separate classrooms." Though much more common today than in previous generations, multiples continue to hold their place of intrigue. Parents of multiples are no stranger to deeply personal questions in the grocery line, stories of grief and tragedy passed along by "a friend of a friend," and well-intentioned, but frequently misguided advice from friends, relatives, and educators. I have come to appreciate these questions and opinions over the years as a way for others to be interested in and participating in my life. While I don't always manage to avoid being annoyed by the questions, I am now more confident in my beliefs and decisions and, as such, care less about others' reactions to my answers.

The truth is that parenting multiples is complex. The "doing" of parenting twins, the how to feed two babies at once or how to get two babies into the car parked 3 flights of stairs and half a parking lot away is a minor challenge. The "being" a parent of twins is an art- it is hard, the way all parenting is, but your decisions feel that much more potent with two intermingled lives being affected by your decisions. How often I have heard parents joke about doing something one way with the first kid and another with the second. When you're doing it twice, at once, it can be unnerving.

Your Expectations of Twins

Everyone reacts to news of expecting twins differently, though I think it is probably safe to say that however one reacts there is a BIG reaction! Whether the news is surprising and a major adjustment or a long-wished-for dream come true, when you find out that you are expecting twins it is likely that you have a picture in your mind of what the future will bring. Perhaps you imagine children who are the closest of confidants and the best of friends. Perhaps you can't imagine how you're going to have enough of you to go around. Perhaps you are thrilled to have siblings to keep each other company. Or, perhaps you are wondering if you are having all of your kids at once.

Whatever your thoughts, expectations, and wonderments about your babies, they most likely say something about your expectation of twins. I have found that parents of twins are actually far more sensitive to fairness and sameness issues than parents of singletons. In fact, I often smile when I see families with singleton kids whose names rhyme or "match" in a way that a parent of multiples agonizes over.

Twin parents need to think about whether they are going to refer to their babies as twins- as in, "the twins are growing out of their clothes." This is in contrast to using the babies individual names- "Mary and Claire are growing out of their clothes." The difference is subtle, but it is present. This subtlety is something that some families might care to highlight and others might not feel it important. Some families enjoy that they have twins- they are proud to call them that and celebrate the bond. The family clearly understands that the twins are different people, and is happy to use their unique relationship as a way to distinguish their children from others. Other families, my own included, prefer to reinforce their children's individuality to the world at large and feel that calling them twins reinforces "unit thinking" for others. They find that using their children's names or saying "my babies" is an important distinction to make. For example, when others ask how old the babies are you might say, "They are nine months old (pause while the person reflects on that information); they are twins." By offering the information that they are twins at the very end, it allows the person the time to look at each child and process them as a unique individual, rather than be viewed from the start as a set.

One of the most prominent "twin-issues" is that of clothing choices- to match, or not to match. The difficulty with this particular topic is that it carries a great deal of baggage for many parents of twins. Some parents of twins enjoy dressing their children alike- literally, just for fun. Many times twins own the same clothes, because friends and family members like buying the babies matching or coordinating sets. Frequently it is just easier- you make one outfit decision and double it! Some parents of multiples specifically don't dress their children alike. Others buy their clothes from stores or sales where matching sets are not available. Some parents of identical twins always try to dress their children in a specific color to assist family and friends with identification. There are really plenty of good reasons to dress your children the same, or different, on any given day.   Because I had boy/girl twins, it was harder to match them and less of an "issue." When they were babies I did tend to dress them in coordinating sleepers- partly because it was cute and partly because it was easier. I never changed one to match the other, however. If someone needed a wardrobe change, only that baby was changed. My babies wore what they had or were given- if it matched it matched and if it didn't, it didn't. As babies, this was enough. To be honest, sometimes I will look back at pictures from my babies early days and I realize all 3 of us are dressed slightly the same- I was just "feeling red" on one day, or "feeling comfy" on another.

My personal opinion about dressing twins alike is like most of my views on parenting. That is, no one way is all bad or all good, probably a combination of the two will make everyone happy. When the babies are little, they are not going to know or care- but will you remember who they are in the pictures looking back? Will you know who they are in the middle of the night when you're still mostly asleep? I will never forget the night I got confused because my daughter was dressed in a blue sleeper my son had outgrown. I couldn't figure out which blue child I had fed- until the other started crying, that is! As the babies get older, they might be of the mind to pick out their own clothes, they might want or not want to be dressed like their sibling...in the same way singleton children might want to match or not match their older or younger siblings. As with all things "twin," flexibility is key. When my children were older and we discussed the issue of dressing-alike, we came up with our very own term- we called it being "double-twins." Just as your children should understand that they are twins, so too should they understand that they are that way whether or not they are dressed the same. Understanding that their bond is one which supersedes clothing, color, and activity preferences can pave the way for individual preferences in the future.

Others Expectations of Twins

Beliefs about twins- who they are, how they behave, and their level of "sameness" is rooted in a person's experience. A person's information about twins necessarily comes from stereotypes- based on media, literary characters, or, more commonly, people they have known or have been with in school. The truth about twins, however, is that you can know as much about any one of them as you would be able to if you were told that they were a girl or a boy or from a certain part of the country or world. Sure, there are trends; there are unique features even to every "twin type," (identical or fraternal, and boys, girls, or both). Knowing that a person is a twin will give you no more information about them than any other random characteristic.

In our culture, however, when people talk about twins, there is an automatic link in our minds to the idea of sameness. That is why strangers ask if they are "boys" or "girls" even though one is clearly dressed in pink and the other in blue. Or, when people find out that a set of twins is a boy and a girl that the next question is "are they identical." There is almost a need, it sometimes appears, to figure out how the babies are "the same." My children are a different gender and they have a different eye color. I can recall many occasions in which I went through step by step conversations about the babies as the person sought to understand how they were the same or different.

>"Are they boys or girls?"
>"I have one of each."
>"Oh, are they identical?"
>"No." (I generally preferred not to get into a genetics lesson)
>"But they have different eye colors"
>"Yes, my son has brown eyes and my daughter has blue eyes."
>"Well what color eyes do you and your husband have...."

And, the conversation generally disintegrated from there. I have had this exact conversation on any number of occasions and I have found these types of conversations to go the most smoothly when I can be factual, non-emotional, and provide no further information than what is requested.

As much as you try to avoid it, you will be asked more questions than you care to answer and frequently this will occur when you very much want to be doing something else. Try, if you can, though, to enjoy the moment and use the time to remember your babies at that moment and look at them the way the curious questioner is looking at them- as the sweetest thing they have seen all day. The moments with your babies are precious and all too often you can speed through the day and wonder at the end of it what you did. Use these moments when others notice your babies to notice them yourself.

As much as others look to define how twins are "the same" they also look to define how they are different and this can be difficult water to wade through. It is amazing how often a parent of multiples is coaxed for information to define their children, in a way that I would argue singletons are less likely to be defined. Children might be described through their interests- one is "artistic" and the other is "sporty." This type of definition, though positive, has potential hazards. Some, unenlightened will ask which one is the "good" twin or the "smart" twin. When these situations arise, my advice is to acknowledge what is true and give a specific example of when it is true. When your babies are little and cannot understand the conversation around them it is important for you to practice handling these types of communications. The way you reframe the query in your answer will help others learn how you view your children and might influence their future conversations with you. When asked about one of your babies personalities it is important to speak of the baby you are discussing by name. Depending on the situation you are in, you can offer a comment on the other baby, or not. For example, if someone asks who the "good sleeper" is, you can say, "They are doing very well. My daughter slept for four hours straight last night and my son has been consistently falling asleep on his own." Do not contradict what the person has said, but instead offer reasons that their observation might be true, albeit in different ways, for both babies.

Comparing Babies

While the casual observer will compare your babies generally, I believe that most of this has to do with clarifying who is who (particularly if they are the same gender, and not exclusively to whether they are identical). Sure, you might hear comments about who is crawling first or how many teeth each baby has, but these comments are superficial and generally observational in nature. The real danger, when it comes to comparing babies, is with the parents themselves.

Many expectant parents begin reading about what is happening with the growth and development of the fetus as they progress week by week through their pregnancy. Parents of multiples, who are often highly monitored and screened, become particularly accustomed to making sure that their babies are hitting appropriate milestones at the right time. "Twenty pounds by twenty weeks" might be a weight-gain target an expectant mother tries to hit. Did she miss that target? Is there a way to catch up? I enjoyed chocolate milkshakes with extra dry milk powder every night as I tried to push the scale to prove my babies were gaining the weight they needed. As a new parent you find yourself in the middle of a game you didn't expect to be playing- one that you would be wise to step out of as soon as you can after your babies are born.

There are two areas of danger for parents of twins. The first is something that all parents fall victim to and only becomes worse for parents of multiples because you have twice (at least) as many children to compare with. This first area of danger is comparing your children to everyone else's. It is virtually impossible to avoid- once you have a baby you begin seeing them everywhere! Strangers strike up conversations with you, drilling you on what your baby has accomplished- sleeping through the night, rolling over, smiling. Friends, good friends even, who mean no harm, trade notes with you about things that have worked or not worked for them. Of course, comparison is human nature, it's one of the ways we figure out if we're doing what we should be doing or trying what we should be trying. It's all fine, unless, it triggers unfounded worry.

The second danger area is perhaps obvious. You have two, or more, children to compare in front of you at all times. One nurses for forty five minutes and the other for twenty, one is sitting up and the other hasn't yet rolled over. At any given minute you have someone to look at and wonder why your other baby has not yet accomplished a similar feat. Remember that there is a range of normal and child development guidelines aim for the average. Your child might not be doing one thing as quickly as a book describes or as their sibling is, but perhaps they are three steps ahead on another task.

There is not much advice to offer when it comes to comparing babies except to try not to. Know that it is a natural tendency and know that the same way each baby gains weight and height on their own timeline, so too, will the developmental tasks be reached. Also remember that your babies adjusted age should be considered when looking at developmental milestones for the first 24 months of life. Even when you think your babies are "caught up," before their first birthday, with everything you believe they should be able to do, you might find that they are walking later, or beginning to talk later than you expect. The role of prematurity cannot be underestimated when it comes to reaching developmental milestones "on time." If you continue to have concerns, you should, of course, make a list and share them with your babies' physician at their next appointment.

"Supersize Me"

Wouldn't it be glorious if there were parenting *sizes*, for just as you can supersize a meal when you're slightly more hungry than usual, so too would we parents of multiples benefit from super-sizing ourselves when our family grows by double at once. We could use a few extra hands to change diapers, an extra chest for sleeping babies to lay on, extra brain power to function on very little sleep, and extra patience to cope with chaos. But this dream is merely that, and the average-sized parent of multiples has to learn to outsmart themselves in order to keep up with the speed of life and needs of babies.

Most people who knew me before twins would have characterized me as an organized person but I think they would all agree that having twins took me to an entirely different level. With twins, I have found that in order for the days and weeks to run the most smoothly you really need to live life about eight steps ahead of yourself. This is an art that I have developed since my babies were born. This level of preparedness does not come naturally, even to those who are born with an innate sense of order. It is, quite seriously, a means of survival for a parent of twins. What this means in practice is that if your babies need to get to a doctor's appointment tomorrow, that you are already preparing today. While this might, overall, seem absurd, I have run into roadblocks more often than not and have lost half-days with seemingly the most innocent and random of issues.

When you think about how to parent twins and how to be a parent of twins you really must consider two areas of growth. First is the actual, physical "doing" of life. These are the "how to clone yourself" questions, like, how to get two babies a bath when you are home alone, how to pick up two crying babies, what to do when the phone rings and your arms are full. You can learn how to do all of these things- either with advice from other parents of multiples, from books, or by trial and error. Never be afraid to try a new idea, and never stop trying new ideas. As your babies grow and develop things will change, sometimes by the hour. What did not work yesterday might work today and what you wish would work today might very well work in a few days if you stick with it. Becoming capable with the tasks of parenting twins is both liberating and confidence-building, two essential traits for your continued journey as a parent. The sooner you make peace with yourself- giving yourself permission to try something new, and not feeling silly if the whole idea fails- the easier you will find the ongoing tasks of parenting twins.

The being a parent of twins is much harder to learn and much more abstract to describe. I have often felt "out of step" with friends and others raising singleton children the same age as my babies. Nothing ever felt quite the same to me as it appeared to be for my friends- the lack of sleep, the ability (or not) to get out of the house. When a parent is already struggling to adapt to their new role, feeling alone in that role can be even more demoralizing. I will never forget the first time I felt this difference square in the face.

My babies were born in the late summer and came home in the early fall. It was a long, cold winter where we did not get out very much. By the time they were around seven months old I was feeling more capable and a more pressing desire to "be normal." I started taking them to a baby playgroup that was held at the library. There was fifteen minutes of songs and stories and then forty five minutes for the babies and parents to interact with toys and each other. I saw, quite quickly, what two babies meant for me. While others picked up their child and moved around the floor, checking out different toys and talking to others while swinging their baby in their arms, I sat on the floor with my babies- in one spot while reaching out to grab a toy here or there that made its way over to our area. I was not mobile in the least, and, as such, I was not social. It's not that others were mean to me, it's just that they were doing what they could do and did not realize my limitations.

We continued attending the playgroup, and talked to those who might be around us. I watched others make coffee dates for afterwards and thought to myself that I wasn't sure my "lunar lander" could even maneuver into or around the coffee shop. I thought that perhaps I was too much work to be friends with, I couldn't zip around with a little stroller, or walk around with one arm full of baby and the other with my hot drink. I wished very much to feel less isolated and wondered if I was having fun.

How did I learn to be a parent of twins? How did I learn to embrace the challenges and enjoy the moments? It was a journey, to be sure. It required building confidence in my parenting decisions both big and small. It required perseverance- attending those playgroups where I felt alone, getting through failed trips to the store, talking myself through the hard days of nursing through growth spurts, and functioning on a severe lack of sleep. It required reaching-out, feeling awkward and uncomfortable at times, and making new friends who were parents of twins. It required an ability to laugh at myself, knowing that there is just nothing that can be done when babies decide to explode through their diapers and spit-up all over at the same time. It requires "digging deep" to find that better self that is there inside of you and accessible only when you want it and need it so badly. I've often heard that things are given only to those who can handle them. Personally, I believe that handling the challenges makes us that person.

When you are expecting twins, or are learning to be the parent of twins, what you must know and remember is this: The road will never be quite as smooth as you might wish and you might never master juggling. But if you remember to love your children and remember that you are doing the very best you can, you will find the energy and strength to get through the day. Each day is the beginning of a new adventure and each adventure will provide a smile once you learn to recognize the moments.

7 JOURNAL: SEPT 25TH, OCT 1ST, 16TH

Sunday, September 25th

The babies were discharged from the hospital on Saturday, September 24th. They were able to show that they could eat enough orally (as opposed to through tube feedings) to gain weight and grow. They'll continue to be followed closely by their doctor and a visiting nurse.

Mom and dad have had a tiresome but wonderful 24 hours as the babies have started to get used to their new home. (Most babies don't have to get used to a NICU and then transition to a new environment- it was much more stressful for them than we imagined!) Everyone is doing well, though, overall, and we're so happy to have them home.

We're only starting to see how tricky it's going to be to take care of two infants, but, we're having fun and have only lost one night's sleep at this point.

We'll provide more updates in the days to come, as we all adjust to the (lack of) schedule a little more. I hear the babies stirring in the background right now- time to eat, again! :)

Love you all- thanks for thinking good thoughts for us.

Saturday, October 1st

(Written by Charlotte and Owen)

Mom and Dad have been so busy and tired that they haven't had a chance to update our webpage... So, we're taking over. :)

We've had a bit of a rough week trying to transition from the hospital NICU environment to home. The sounds, lights, schedule, and overall space are different. It's a lot to take in and can get very upsetting at times. Owen, in particular, has a lot of trouble at night and needs to be held quite a bit. While we were swaddled together in the hospital, we've been so upset overnight that we've been disturbing each other here at home. Mom and dad can't seem to figure out why every morning when they went into the hospital the nurses said we had a great night- now they're happy if we get a great hour! We haven't done the best job sleeping at the same time overnight so they're up pretty much the whole time.

In the meantime, Dad has to go back to work on Monday so they've been trying to figure out how he's going to be able to sleep and function at work during our overnight parties! Partly we're still not doing the best job eating which makes for some long attempts at feeding overnight. Sometimes we're just too tired to nurse, so we fall asleep quickly and wake up hungry very shortly afterwards, or we're just so disorganized that we can't seem to figure out what we're supposed to do to eat!

We're still combining breast feeding & bottle feeding (of milk mom has pumped). It's a lot of work for her and she's sure everything will be a whole lot easier when we can nurse (ideally at the same time) and not worry about bottles, heating up milk, and pumping every time we want to eat. She's much happier because we were pretty successful nursing during the day today.

We continue to sleep or eat most of the day- not much play time yet! We're so excited to meet all of mom and dad's friends and family. We're so little, though, and not supposed to be here date-wise until October 19th. The doctors want us to stay away from people and out of public for the first two months (3 weeks down). If we get sick at all during this time, we could get very sick and will need a lot of tests.

Mom and Dad are dying to show us off and it's taking all their self control to "obey" directions. Thanks to all of you who want to come visit and cuddle with us. We promise, we're so little that when our immune system is finally up to speed that we'll still be cute as anything and will throughly enjoy visiting with everyone!

We'll keep you posted on how we're doing, though, and can't wait to meet you all!

Love, Owen and Charlotte

Thursday, October 6th

Owen and Charlotte are growing by ounces, which, at their size is like leaps and bounds. Everyday is an adventure in keeping up with feedings, diapers, and necessary wardrobe changes. Lots of details to manage in terms of figuring out how to do 8 things at once, with never enough hands.

Last night mom actually got 2, 2-hour stretches of sleep and wow what a difference that made! We're hoping that they can keep that up on a more consistent basis. Nights are still hard for the babies and they need a lot of TLC throughout the night. But, they're still not supposed to be here yet, so we have to keep perspective.

Still having tons of fun- despite the fatigue. It only takes a cute look from one of the babies to make all of it worth while.

8 THE EARLY DAYS AT HOME

I remember leaving the hospital with my two tiny babies- I think I remember this because there was a picture of us doing so. I do remember the few minute drive home feeling like it might actually be taking several hours. I also remember bringing the babies into the apartment for the very first time and laying them down on blankets on the floor. I think the feeling that has remained with me from that moment is one of peace. The babies were finally mine. It was quiet.

Let's be real, all hell had not yet broken loose and I had no idea what would happen next. I actually don't remember much about that afternoon or evening. I'm sure I fed them- I started trying to breastfeed right away when I came home. Because they were so tiny, and had no head control, in the beginning I literally needed an extra set of hands to get them to latch. It was quite a process, but the truth is, what wasn't in those early days!

I cannot say that I know any twin parents who were able to sleep that first night that the babies were home. I do have rather clear memories of "putting the babies to bed." I also remember laying down in my bed at least once. I have no memory of sleeping at all.

First of all, to be clear, the babies have no idea that it is nighttime and that you would prefer to be sleeping. They are just as hungry and tired as they are at any other moment of a 24-hour day. They will sleep for varying periods of time, and not necessarily the same periods of time as their twin. Whether your babies were premature or full-term, you likely have months of practice ahead of you so don't worry if the first night home is a disaster!

If your babies are making a second transition from NICU to home, I would suggest reading any paperwork you were sent home with sooner rather than later. I remember pulling out the hospital discharge paperwork and pamphlets a week or two after we came home and realizing that they would have been helpful in knowing what to expect. Everything from the level of noise and lights to the ability or desire to stay on the NICU schedule will affect the babies, and, as a result, you.

There is so much to learn, understand, and work through when it comes to meeting the feeding and sleeping needs of multiple infants. Even if you are already a parent, addressing these needs for multiples is an entirely different affair. Figuring out what your babies need from you and how best to help them is going to be a long term process. I promise, no matter how prepared you are, you will not figure it out the very first night.

To make it through the first nights, let me suggest reorienting your thinking from "day-night" to "sleeping-not sleeping." While we once previously assumed that "morning" meant it was time to get up, get dressed, and have a day, now I would suggest that you just continue going back to sleep- every time the babies do, for as long into the day as your body will let you. I used to consider it a "win" if I put real clothes on by noon. One of the most important tasks for you and your spouse is to get as much rest as possible while caring for your babies. Later chapters on feeding and sleeping will provide more tools for successful nights.

Clocks

There's a saying about time and whether it is "on your side." Before you had babies you probably would agree that there was never enough of it, or that you didn't know what to do with it. When you're pregnant you anxiously await the arrival of your babies- hoping that you'll make it to term, planning ahead for an early arrival, bed rest, or medical complications that require an extended hospitalization. It seems as though from the moment you realize that a baby (or two!) is due, you begin a countdown. You start thinking about rearranging your house, figuring out what equipment and stuff you need, and planning events, travels, baby showers, and employment situations for a brief (or not so brief) hiatus. Once those twins arrive, however, I promise that your trouble with time will only intensify.

When I was pregnant I read some advice about not looking at the clock throughout the night when you are getting up. The idea was that it wasn't going to change whether or not you got up, and would instead serve to reinforce your fatigue, help you count how many times you got up, etc. I took this to heart and, in fact, moved a clock away from my bed and into the kids room. When I heard crying I just got up and went into the room, fed, changed, and settled, and went back to bed. I didn't focus on whether or not I had been up only an hour before that, and didn't focus on how long it took to get through things. I credit this advice for significantly helping my mental status during those early months of fatigue. This advice provided me with the mental framework I needed to cope with the tangled mess of time that I was in. I had a clear understanding that I had job and it had to get done. The time on the clock did not matter, and the idea that counting minutes would just reinforce my fatigue made sense. This was a really important part of managing my mindset in the early weeks.

Taking Care of Babies

There are only a limited number of tasks that are truly required to care for your babies each day. The biggest of these- feeding and sleeping- have so many nuances, that they have their own dedicated sections of this book. This section, then, covers more general needs, like diapering, bathing, and general supplies that make your life easier. It is my hope that what you will come away from this section with is an appreciation for lowered expectations as a means of survival!

Clothing: When I was little I used to change my doll's clothes constantly. I laugh now, thinking of it, as my own real babies got their clothes changed when they were dirty, or wet, and not much in between. As an adult who slept every night and woke up each morning to get ready for the day, it honestly didn't occur to me that my babies would not function in the same way! I mean, I knew babies woke up throughout the night to eat, but I didn't quite grasp that there would be no definition of day and night for me for quite a while. I quickly learned that I was living in a never-ending loop and there was no beginning or end to any day. This is when I started changing the babies clothes when they needed it rather than in the mornings, as I previously presumed one would. I changed my own clothes in the same way- changing my t-shirt when it needed it, and throwing my shirts into the laundry right with the babies! I did use baby-specific detergent on their clothes as well as my own shirts, as the babies faces would be snuggled up against them. We learned early on that our babies had sensitive skin and we used the most gentle formula we could to avoid further issues. As they grew, their skin seemed to get a little tougher as well and we switched over to regular detergent around their first birthday.

Diapering: In general you'll know when your babies need their diapers changed, and the truth is that you will likely be kept so busy feeding them and getting them up and down from sleep that you will not have a lot of extra time to "check" in between. In the early weeks, especially, you'll likely change them before or after they eat. You may want to change them before they eat so that they're all fresh and clean while you hold them. But, there are some interesting reflexes that come factory installed, and you may find out that shortly into eating your babies might make room for more, shall we say! If you find this to be the case, you may want to plan on changing them at the end of eating!

One of the ways that parents are taught to make sure their babies are eating enough is by the number of wet and dirty diapers that the babies have. What we did each night was to set a pile out that contained a certain number of diapers- at the end of the day we could see exactly how many we had gone through. Now, this isn't an exact science. Of course it relies on the parents having a general feel about whether both babies were changed on a similar schedule or whether one was slightly more or less than average. In general, however, if you're not specifically worried about one baby, this should work well enough.

Bathing: I had a twin mom friend whose twins were her second and third children. She was talking with me one day about bedtime and about how exhausting it was. I then found out that she was bathing all of her children daily. I made a joke at the time about how she might not know this, being the parent of a singleton, but that "twins did not need baths everyday." While partially noted in jest, the truth remains that bathing twins is a lot of work. Speaking for myself, we were generally unsuccessful at a "Hollywood" bath experience. My babies could care less about baths, generally, so, in the wrong mood, they hated them! Someone was always wet, someone was cold, and, as parents, we were always rushing to fit it in before someone was hungry or tired. If both parents were available bath time went much more smoothly. If there was only one adult, the baby in the bouncy chair was always upset. We used an inexpensive baby bathtub that could fit in our kitchen sink- it was what worked best in our apartment. Despite all the work, I must admit that there are few things better than snuggling with a clean baby in a fleecy sleep sack!

Supplies

There are plenty of lists available that offer suggestions about the types of supplies and gear that are "essential" for baby. As a family on a limited budget and with limited space I like to think we stuck with the true essentials. So much baby gear is available both new and used. You will want to do your research and make sure you understand what the current safety recommendations are before you purchase any products. Mom-2-Mom Sales (particularly sponsored by local twins groups) are a great place to locate gear in duplicate!

Here's what I recommend:

Car Seats- One for each baby.

This is probably the only piece of required baby equipment and your babies will not be released from the hospital unless you have an appropriate child seat. There are so many options on the market and all have specific height and weight guidelines. A few words of advice. First, remember that your babies may be born early and may be little. You may want to ensure that your seat will hold babies under eight pounds. If they are super-tiny the hospital should be able to help you rent a car-bed for them, but keep in mind that they might be little for a while. For this reason we chose to get an infant-only seat as our first seat and later got a convertible seat that they used for much longer. Second, remember there are actually two important measurements- weight and length. I was under the impression that weight limits were the only factor I needed to consider, but my little premies grew out of their car seat by length far sooner than they would have hit the weight limit. Make sure you note both of those numbers when you compare car seat options. Finally, especially when you're having twins, it is really helpful to be able to snap your babies' car seats right into the stroller. If you can get a travel system with a compatible stroller it is especially helpful in those early months!

Stroller-

I was a one-stroller-mama for a long time. I found the front to back double stroller that would accept two infant car seats to be the right choice for me. Be careful when looking, not all double strollers are designed to accept two infant car seats. Some are designed for multiple age children and will only accept one infant car seat. There was a good storage basket underneath the seats in our stroller which held the large diaper bag. I found the front to back design to be easy enough to maneuver inside stores, through door frames, and down the sidewalk. We happily used this one stroller until the babies were 18-months-old and the airline temporarily broke the stroller. While we waited for replacement parts we purchased two nice single strollers as well as a very inexpensive connector set that made the singles into a double side-by-side. For at least the first year, and generally later on when I had the babies out on my own, I found the double travel-system-stroller to be the perfect fit for us.

Cribs- One for each baby.

Even if they start out sleeping together, you will likely want them to have their own space at some point in the future. There are not many kids who enjoy taking naps and for that time alone you may want them in isolation! Depending on the set up of your home and the potential for travel you may also wish to have a portable crib set up of some kind, one for each baby. There are a number of different kinds on the market and the market is always changing. There are benefits to many of the options and you'll have to pick the option that makes sense for your particular needs.

Bouncy Seats- One for each baby.

While my babies did not like sitting by themselves, they much preferred hanging out in people's arms or in carriers, there are times when they must be put down somewhere safe and I found a bouncy seat (ideally with a handle so you can carry it, with the baby in it, into another space) to be just the thing. At some point you may want a shower (two of these seats can fit even in the tiniest of apartment bathrooms), or may want to cook dinner, or may just need a place to put one baby while you bathe or change the other. My kids enjoyed the seats that played music and vibrated- a little distraction from the idea that they hated being alone!

Carriers- One for each baby.

We preferred the front carriers with lumbar back support (especially important as the babies put on weight). The carriers could be used when the babies were as little as 8 lbs with them facing us and could be used when the babies were bigger, had head control, and could face forward. The kind of carrier we used had the ability to be cinched as tight as we needed- we had both hands free and that baby wasn't going to go anywhere!

Nursing Pillow- One designed for twins.

If I had to pick only one piece of baby equipment that would of made the most difference in my child care life, this would be it. I think it is worth every penny. More information about the benefits of this item can be found in the chapter about breastfeeding.

Floor Mat Gyms- One for each baby- same or different designs as you prefer.

While this is clearly an optional item, it is something that my babies spent tons of time on and with throughout their first year. They napped on the floor on the mats, they enjoyed batting the toys while they laid on their back, they enjoyed a whole new experience with the gym when they learned to sit up. This was where they spent their tummy time and where I could lay the babies next to each other on the floor together. I would lay one baby in each gym and somehow they would finagle their way over to the other! If your gym has a toy that perhaps lights up and sings, I promise you that many years later you will still occasionally have dreams where the toys are all singing, just a little out of sync!

Swaddling Blankets- A bunch.

These were really helpful in the beginning when we always put our babies to sleep in a swaddle. There are all kinds of swaddling products out there, but the truth is that we just used square blankets- you get good at swaddling really quickly when it works! We were also sent home from the hospital with some double-sized swaddling blankets so that we could swaddle the babies together at home the way we did in the hospital. I believe these blankets were specially made and donated to the hospital. If you have a seamstress in your life, perhaps they could whip up a couple for you (dimensions approximately 42 inches square)

Burp Cloths- A TON.

Maybe your babies won't spit up a lot at first, but at some point they probably will (particularly when they really get the eating thing down and start gulping!), and you will go through a lot of burp cloths each day. I used them throughout the day, for everything. I laid them under the babies heads no matter where they were laying so that if they drooled or spit up some milk that I didn't have to figure out how to clean something bigger. Along these lines, there are lap pads and absorbent sheets that you can tie over your crib sheets- all of these are helpful for the same reason!

Sleepers & Sleep Sacks- Plenty, both in light and heavy fabrics depending on where you live and the season in which your babies will be born.

As I mentioned earlier about clothing changes- they didn't happen at regular intervals, though did happen frequently enough. My babies lived in "sleep and plays" of all sorts. They were easy to put on, easy to wash, and covered the babies toes without dealing with socks! We also loved the sleep sacks. Because we live in a cold climate we would layer a lighter weight sleep sack inside of a heavy fleece sleep sack in the winter. There is nothing more cozy than a little fleecy ball of baby!

Diapers-

Whether you are trying to use cloth or disposable, you will likely want several kinds to try out with your babies. We found that different brands fit in different ways and that some were just cut to fit our babies better. There are many opinions out there about which options are better for the environment, better for the wallet, and easiest to use. You will have to research each options' costs and benefits and think about how it will fit into your life. Depending on your childcare situation, laundry machine situation, storage ability, etc, one option might be preferable. Because we were in an apartment with coin laundry we did not have the laundry situation necessary for personal cloth diapers nor the storage ability necessary for a double supply of clean and dirty diapers from a diaper service. For us, disposable diapers, that could be frequently disposed of in the dumpsters at our complex, were the right choice. I have many twin-mom-friends who have successfully used all of the above-mentioned options. Twins does not preclude you from any particular diapering method!

Also remember that you can change your mind. If you want to start one way and, two months in, you realize that that way isn't working or you think the other way now looks more appealing, check it out. Flexibility, with all things "twin," is key. Regardless of the overall method you choose, I recommend having a back-up package of disposables available for emergencies- these emergencies might range from the personal (like a baby's need for a round of antibiotics and their subsequent change in elimination patterns) to the environmental (such the power going out for a few days after a storm leaving you with no way to start your washing machine).

Bottles-

Whether you plan on breast or bottle feeding, I recommend checking out the bottle options and either purchasing a starter set or knowing what you would want and having it written down for whomever might need to pick it up for you after the babies are born. So much about your plans can change depending on how early the babies are and being prepared for all eventualities is helpful. I had a bottle set that was very flexible- the tops could be changed out and used throughout the babies lives- with nipples as bottles, with valved tops as "sippy-cups," and with flat covers to hold snacks. I used my set with all of those options and got my money's worth despite the fact that I eventually exclusively breastfed.

Breast Pump-

Like bottles, a breast pump may be required whether or not you intend it to be. More specific information about choosing a pump can be found in the "Feeding Infants" chapter. Like bottles, I suggest having one picked out, with the name written down so that you can send someone out to purchase it if and when you need it. Breast pumps are an investment and I generally recommend waiting to see how things go before purchase.

High Chairs- One for each baby.

You will eventually begin to feed your baby solid food and at this time you will want to have a safe place for them to sit upright and make a mess. There are so many varieties of chairs that will help you feed your baby, but you will likely want something that will work for them when they are self-feeding. Because we did not have lot of space, we actually did not have room for the babies at a table of any kind, so the regular, full-size highchairs were the right choice for us. We preferred ones with a 5-point harness (so that when they get older and start leaning over the side you know they're contained), wheels, so I could drag the chairs right where I needed them with the babies in them, and multiple trays that snapped on top of the main tray (so that when I didn't have time to clean them between meals I could just pop off the dirty tray and pop a clean one on). And, upon advice from various high chair reviews, we also looked for trays that had the release lever in the front where only I could reach it, rather than on the sides where the babies would eventually be able to reach.

Diaper Bag-

I had two diaper bags that I tried to keep packed at all times. I had a large one, that held a good day's worth of supplies- 5 or 6 diapers per baby, an extra change of clothes per baby, burp cloths, and food/snack/bottle supplies we might need, and various "extra" items like plastic baggies for dirty diapers, hand sanitizer, and a notepad and pen to aid my non-existent memory. I also had a small diaper bag that was packed for more of an hour or two trip out- a few diapers, a few burp clothes, a few mom-essentials, etc. It is always important to have at least one of these bags with you at all times and, on the occasion that your babies might be in two different locations, you have a bag ready to go with each child.

Adjusting to Life with Two Babies

There are so many adjustments that you are making in the early days with your babies at home. Both parents are adjusting to their new roles individually and as a parenting team. Mother's bodies are attempting to recover from a traumatic number of months. Nothing feels the same as it used to, and frankly, you might still feel so big or full of fluid that you're still being asked if you are pregnant! There is so much to figure out and manage during the day. The key to staying sane is to cut yourself some slack. Things are not going to go smoothly, perhaps any day. You will feel overwhelmed as your responsibilities have exponentially multiplied. But know that you will figure it out. Each "bad day," goodness, each "bad hour" will help you learn what is working (or not) for your family. There is no one solution that will work for everyone and trial and error works better than you may imagine when it comes to figuring out how to best parent your infants.

Try to go slow; try to stay calm in an crazy environment. Know that your babies cry because that is all they know how to do to communicate. It does not mean that they are hurt, it does not mean you are a bad parent, it just means they wish for something different- whether that is a clean diaper, or a snack, or to be held, or to fall asleep. The options are really very few in the early weeks- and that is a good thing for parents! I promise that you will get used to working under pressure. You will get used to staying peppy and calm for the babies through their protests. You will find that you can help them feel better, and you should draw strength from your successes. Every day will not be a good one, and some will be harder than others. Sometimes you will need to cry right along with the babies. Sometimes you will need to call your own mom or a friend who understands to cry to them. But, I also promise that the next time those babies are asleep at the same time, and you've had a chance to take a shower and put on a clean shirt, if you sneak over and look at those two peaceful cherubs that you would do the whole horrible day right over again.

9 JOURNAL: OCT 23RD

Sunday, October 23rd

How many times I've thought about writing a little update... and how many times I've been distracted on the way to the computer! The little cherubs (as we like to call them) are currently sleeping, though Owen likes to eat every two hours...and he's pretty much like clockwork. So, as I figure it, I've got about 4 minutes left!

Everyone is doing well. We can't believe the babies are 6 weeks old today. Of course, we remind ourselves that we've only had them home for 4 weeks. Last night the twins graced me with the gift of 3 hours from start of feed to start of feed- which means we got a few sets of 2 hours to sleep.

Owen and Charlotte continue to spend most of the day eating and sleeping. We can now say that they've reached their due date which was last Wednesday (October 19th). When they are awake, we have fun guessing whether an adorable smile or coo is actually a response to us, or, an involuntary expression! We like to think the former, of course. The babies are starting to explore their world a little more. Every now and then they hit a toy on their little vibrating chairs or floor mat gyms and we again have to decide whether it was purposeful or not. We're pretty sure that it is...about 50% of the time. :)

Mom and dad are surviving- getting things under control a little more everyday. It's a good day when everyone is up, cleaned up, and dressed by noon. Hey, that's a feat when you have to eat every two hours and it takes about an hour to get the whole ordeal over with!

Well, my 4 minutes are up! The overall message- we're still having fun and loving every minute of being parents.

10 FEEDING INFANTS

One of the few things you come home from the hospital with a head start on is feeding your babies. How much experience you receive, and how well it goes likely depends on how long you are admitted, how long your babies are admitted, how knowledgable and supportive the nursing staff are about breastfeeding, how available lactation consultants are, and, how early your babies were born. You will come home feeding your babies either by bottle, by breast, or by a combination of the two. This chapter will cover nursing, pumping, and bottle feeding, as different combinations of these feeding options are right for each family. Because twin-specific breastfeeding requires a special art, the majority of the chapter will focus on those nuances.

Making the Decision: Breast or Bottle

Breastfeeding can be a wonderful experience. It is a time for you and your babies to be together and it is a way for you to feel connected to them. Breastfeeding's health benefits for both mother and baby have been well documented. Once mom and babies get the process down, it is a lot easier than formula feeding- less formula to prepare, less bottles to wash, and less money by a landslide!

Breastfeeding twins is no easy task, especially in the early weeks at home. That being said, it is very possible to be successful and to have an amazing experience. I would argue that the single most important variable involved in success is the mother's desire to breastfeed. This is not a job for the weak at heart- it requires an iron will and an impressive determination. Feeling like "you'll see how it goes" probably isn't determined enough if you really want to make it work. It is a tough job- it is constant, it can be painful at times (when nipples are sore or teeth are coming in), and it is fatiguing. Success at breastfeeding, though, offers a confidence boost like no other in parenting.

The most important points to keep in mind:
- Exclusively nursing twins is entirely possible.
- You can produce enough milk for two (or more) babies.
- You can transition from hospital bottle feeding to exclusive nursing.
- You should nurse, or not, based on what is right for you and your family.

Exclusive breast feeding does not work for every mother for a variety of reasons. Knowing yourself and what you feel able to manage and comfortable with is very important. Some babies are hospitalized after birth in the neonatal intensive care unit. These babies might be unable to breastfeed, possibly at all, initially. These babies might need time to grow and develop; they might need to learn how to "suck, swallow, breath." Mom might be ready to be discharged from the hospital prior to her babies, so she might not always be around to feed them when they are hungry. For mothers whose babies don't get started with breastfeeding right away, the road can be more more difficult when they get home. This does not mean you cannot breastfed, or that you cannot exclusively breastfeed. It just means that it will be a little bit more difficult to get to the ultimate goal. If your babies come home using bottles for any or all of their feedings, as long as you are still pumping regularly (aim for every two hours even throughout the night) you can transition them to breastfeeding.

Some babies need extensive medical care after birth and are hospitalized for a long time. It can be a struggle for mothers to keep up with what is happening with their babies and pump as much as is required to build and maintain a milk supply. This can cause too much stress at a time when your body and mind is already so strained. For these mothers, and any mother who does not have the desire to breastfeed, it should be specifically stated that having yourself in the best mental place you can is the single most important part of caring for your newborn babies. The right way to feed your babies is the way you can do it and maintain your sanity, your energy, and your ability to enjoy these fleeting moments with your newborns. Once you make the decision that you are not going to breastfeed, you must make peace with yourself and move forward without guilt. Two very beautiful babies need your attention and love and those are the feelings you must embrace. You will find others who have made the same decision as you, whatever that is, and they will be an enormous source of support for you as you move forward caring for your babies.

BREASTFEEDING

How and Where to Sit

Here's how I found success with breastfeeding. First, the best money I spent on baby gear was for a special "twin-specific" nursing pillow. It had a back support and a wider platform than most Boppie-style pillows. It was also cut at an angle so that it slanted towards my body, causing the babies to roll towards me rather than off the side of the pillow. It also had a strap so that I could literally synch it tight around my waist. This pillow was an essential part of making breastfeeding work. I felt that both babies were safe and would not roll off, so I was hands-free when they were older and could hold their latch. I became so comfortable with this arrangement, actually, that I became very good at finagling all three of us- so that I could sit at my desk with my knees under the front two corners of the pillow and type while they were nursing. I could also pick them up, while they were nursing, by holding the sides of the pillow to move around on the couch or grab the telephone. In fact, my very first Thanksgiving dinner with the babies was eaten at the table- with them happily latched and nursing.

Where you nurse depends on what type of pillow and gear set up you prefer. Most twin nursing pillows are too wide for a standard glider and even for most recliner chairs. I found the best place to nurse was the couch. I would strap on my twin nursing pillow and sit towards the middle of the couch. I would place one baby at a time on the couch, on either side of where I was going to sit. Once seated, I would pull each baby onto the pillow. Now, if others are home and can hand you the babies while you're already sitting that is even easier! When I sat down to nurse I planned to be there for a while. I had a small side table right near my nursing station that had the television remote, the telephone, a water bottle and a snack (more on that in a minute).

Together or Separate

While I know moms who always nursed one baby at a time, the truth is that you can easily spend every moment nursing. And, when I say every moment, I truly mean just that. It is entirely possible that you will feel you spend every moment nursing when you tandem nurse as well! Regardless of what you ultimately find to be the right system for you, my recommendation is to master tandem feeding first and then decide how you prefer to nurse the babies long-term.

In addition to the very significant time savings of tandem nursing there are actually other benefits worth noting. In the early days, especially, when the babies are still learning to nurse, you may find that one baby is more efficient and gets the hang of nursing more quickly. If they are tandem feeding, both babies can benefit from either one of them being able to trigger a let-down. In those first days and weeks when many parents and physicians are watching the babies' weight gains very closely, the easier it is to get the liquid gold that is breast milk into the babies, the better.

Along these same lines, in the early days when my body was still becoming accustomed to all of the tasks of nursing I could not feel the let down, I also could not stop the milk flow from a side not in use. For anyone who has nursed or pumped, "wasted" breast milk is definitely worth crying over. I found it much more efficient to let the milk flow and have the babies be fed all at the same time.

Finally, whether a sentimental wish or an accurate observation, my babies loved to be on that nursing pillow together. We found that no matter how far apart they were when they started, when they were done nursing they were both asleep, head to head and hand in hand. There is no sweeter memory that I have of my babies than that image.

Getting the Latch

In the early days and weeks, how long depending on how early your babies were born, you will have to help the babies latch and you may need to continue to hold their heads while they are nursing. Having a second adult you feel comfortable with helping you to hold a baby's head will allow you to nurse the babies at the same time. There are a few key points with regard to getting your babies to latch the right way. First, it should not hurt. If it hurts, you should gently place your finger on the side of their mouth and "pop them off" as I used to say. While it might seem annoying to you and frustrating to the baby in the beginning, it is essential to get the latch right now. Improperly latched babies will cause pain when nursing and can cause major nipple soreness that is slow to go away.

For premies and those who may have needed a combination of bottles and breast, getting a good latch can be difficult. I used a nipple shield for both babies. This small plastic shield looks a bit like a sewing thimble and fits over your nipple. The shields come in multiple sizes, so make sure you get one that will be comfortable. The idea of the nipple shield is that as the baby sucks, your nipple will get pulled up into the thimble portion of the plastic and milk will flow. The nipple shield provides a more rigid structure for the baby to latch onto, increasing their chances of a good latch.

The nipple shield can provide protection for sore and broken down skin. It can also, however, put increased pressure on the nipple as it gets pulled up into the shield. Essentially, it is a tool- to be used if it makes life easier and to be weaned off of when possible (because that will ultimately make your life easier!). The shield is wet with milk at the end of a nursing session and requires one more hand and burp cloth around to help with.

Nursing

How long your babies nurse will depend entirely on the babies. Some babies are very efficient- they eat quickly and lose interest. Others relax and can alternate between sleeping and eating for forty five minutes to an hour at a time. Some babies suck in a lot of air while they nurse and need to be burped frequently. Others can explode through their diapers shortly into a nursing session with surprising regularity. Expect the unexpected and plan for nothing and you'll do fine.

Nursing babies generally eat every few hours. My son was like an atomic clock and you could pretty much tell the time down to his cry for food. He liked to eat every two hours, and, his sister was therefore put on his schedule. Some babies space out their feedings over time, and others, like my son, preferred to keep up the every two hour deal for months on end. Some times of day are more difficult. There is something about the late afternoon and early evening- babies just get cranky! My babies were known to cluster feed during that time- they might eat every hour or so during that early evening, before falling asleep for what was generally their longest stretch. This, of course, generally coincided with the time my husband might be home and our chance to talk for a few minutes, making it difficult for me to get inspired to go to sleep as I should!

Generally speaking, I recommend "on demand" feeding for twins. The truth is that I found that someone was always (it seemed) hungry and I generally fed the other baby at the same time. I did my best to have a little time "off" between feedings, but I didn't stress out about it. They had plenty of opportunities to eat and it seemed more humane to offer food when they cried than to wait a given amount of time. There are plenty of books that offer suggested schedules, and plenty of families that try to keep their babies on the hospital schedule (every three hours for us) when the babies come home. This might work for some families, but it did not work for mine.

Breastfed babies, generally, take in less air then bottle-fed babies. You should, though, slow down the nursing and burp your babies periodically- especially if they seem to be eating quickly. If you are tandem nursing, the easiest way to burp a baby is to leave one latched and nursing while sitting the other up, on the nursing pillow, leaned against your shoulder. You can then gently pat or rub the baby's back until they burp. Get the baby settled, re-latched, and nursing before you attempt to burp the other baby.

Who Ate Where

There are a few ways to handle the "who eats where" question. Some mothers assign one side to each baby and that baby eats there all of the time. Mothers who choose this system like that each baby has a chance to get the, more filling, hind milk as they feed the same baby off of the same side all of the time. They also do not need to remember anything more. Other mothers choose a variation of this theme and have each baby on one side for a day at a time, figuring that it is easier to remember, but hoping to keep milk production (and therefore breast size) more similar. Finally, some mothers (and I am among them) prefer to switch sides virtually every feeding.

I felt there were a number of benefits to switching every feeding. First, I felt like my milk supply was in constant use. It's much harder, though not impossible, to get clogged ducts when you're being literally sucked dry throughout the day! Second, I felt like my milk supply had more time to "keep up" when the hungrier baby would get the "more full" breast on the next feeding. Now, there were times, of course, when one baby didn't seem hungry and clearly didn't do justice on their share of a certain breast. On those occasions, at the next feeding I did NOT switch sides as I wanted the baby who hadn't had their fill to have a very full breast and an easy time nursing. Milk production, and breast size, was consistent across the sides, which looked and felt more comfortable to me.

The only downside of this approach was remembering who ate where last. If I had a nickel for every time I called out to my husband, "who was on what side?" we'd have their college fund well started. It was only later, after I had finished nursing that I saw some charms for sale in a parenting magazine. They were designed to hook onto your bra strap and were reminiscent of "wine charms," so that one could identify their wine glass at a party. They were cute, with little pink or blue beads on them. Though not designed for parents of multiples, they certainly would have been helpful! You really only need one charm which you would associate with one baby to switch back and forth and you would have to be consistent about when you switched the charm- perhaps when the babies first start eating- so you know which side they will be on later. This is an example of one of those little ideas that is so hard to come up with when you're in the moment. Once a brilliant idea like this becomes obvious, it is easy to generalize. You don't really need to buy anything- use a bracelet or a hairband and switch wrists at every feeding. Relying on something other than your brain is a very good idea for parents of twins.

How you hold your babies, on their chosen side, has only to do with your comfort. Other than overnight, when I used a side-lying position, I nursed my babies almost exclusively with a double football hold. This positioning was the easiest to use with the nursing pillow, and was, therefore, the easiest for me. Because I switched babies and sides each feeding, more or less, they were both accustomed to feeding laying either direction. On occasion I might have one baby nursing laying opposite their usual. I had read that pointing the babies chin towards an area that feels clogged is helpful. There were times, then, that I had one baby laying on top of the others legs as I tried to massage out a painful duct.

Who Ate What

We came home from the hospital with handy little charts to record nursing sessions and diaper changes. It is generally the first weeks, when the doctors are still watching the babies' weights, that these charts are the most important. The problem with the charts, however, is that you have to remember to fill them in. I was notoriously bad at remembering to write anything down. My husband and mother did as best they could to pick up my slack in the early days, but I never did get any better. I just had too many babies always in my hands and I was sitting behind the nursing pillow for so many hours that I barely remembered to eat and go to the bathroom myself! If you can remember to write down your nursing sessions- particularly remembering how long each baby ate, great. As technology advances rapidly, "apps" are now available on smart phones so that easier options for tracking baby care are available. Whatever your method, remember that outsmarting yourself is the key to successful early days!

Switching from Bottle to Breast

My babies came home from the hospital mostly bottle-feeding. They had had the opportunity to try to nurse, generally once or twice a day only and were not strong enough to try more than that. I timed my visits to the hospital so that they would line up with as many feedings as possible (the hospital kept them on a schedule) but some days my babies were too tired to nurse, as it is more difficult for them than bottle-feeding. After coming home we immediately began tandem nursing and then supplemented with bottles of pumped milk after each nursing session. I won't lie, it was an enormous amount of work. In the first days we had family around, and they were able to assist with bottles after each nursing session so that I could go and pump. Between nursing and pumping there was very little time left in the day. As the days and weeks went on, and the babies were able to demonstrate that they were holding or gaining weight we were able to start dropping supplemental feedings. We began by dropping the overnight bottles, one at a time, and then the daytime bottles. As long as we were bottle feeding I continued pumping and we used fresh milk- both to keep my supply in line with what the babies were eating, and because it was easier than thawing and freezing. The supply that was in the freezer stayed there during this time.

With the help of the nipple shield and quite a bit of patience, we were gradually able to transition to exclusive breastfeeding. Oh what an accomplishment it was. And, after all of the supplemental-feedings, bottle washing, pump part washing, constant nursing and pumping, and tears over each challenge it was incredibly satisfying. For me, successfully breastfeeding was really important. I felt as though I had lost all control throughout my pregnancy and delivery. Both of those experiences were dramatically different than I ever expected them to be, and not always in a positive way. At the time, I felt like breastfeeding was my last chance to possibly have an experience that felt incredibly important to me.

Keeping Mom Fed

An often overlooked part of successful breastfeeding is keeping mom hydrated and nourished. As with any manufacturing facility, keeping the raw materials plentiful is essential for production. So too with moms, who require food and water to make breast milk. Remembering to drink enough water is as important now, if not more so, than it was was when you were pregnant and trying to prevent preterm labor. In order to make sure this happened I used little plastic water bottles, which were refilled daily for me by my husband. Every time I nursed I drank an entire water bottle. You might think you would just pour a glass of water, or that you'll grab a drink after you nurse, but you won't. Someone will need a diaper, someone else will be asleep and need to be carried to their crib. Once you've placed the babies in their cribs you'll remember that you haven't used the bathroom all morning, and then you notice that your shirt has spit-up on it and you need to change it. When you're in the bedroom changing your shirt you'll realize that the bed looks so inviting, and you'll lay down, just for a minute. The next thing you know someone is crying and it's time to nurse again... and you have not had a drink. So, do yourself a favor, and grab a water bottle every time you are carrying babies over to the couch (even every time overnight) and drink the entire bottle while you're nursing. Then you will be ready for whatever happens next.

Of course eating a well-balanced diet, as you did in pregnancy, is preferred while you are nursing. Vitamins, nutrients, fresh fruit and vegetables- it's all good for your body, and, therefore, your breast milk. But let's be reasonable- on some days you will be lucky to change your shirt, you are not going to fix yourself a salad for lunch. The important thing is to remember to eat something! In the first weeks of breastfeeding especially, I made it my mission to eat a snack along with each water bottle that I faithfully downed. While I am not one to generally purchase prepackaged snacks, I found that this is entirely the right time to do it. Just as you will find it difficult to fill a glass with water, so too will it sometimes seem impossible to pour a bowl of cereal. Individual, prepackaged snacks like granola bars, pudding, applesauce, string cheese, and even cereal boxes will be a huge help to you. Have a pile of them in the kitchen that you can grab when you grab your water bottle and eat a snack each time you nurse. Or, store the non-perishables right next to the couch so that you can always grab a bite when you're hungry, or when you realize you don't remember when you last ate. Finally, when you do eat meals, make sure you are eating enough good fats- when you are establishing your milk supply and trying to fatten up your babies you can and should make sure you have enough yourself.

Other's Expectations about Breastfeeding

Breastfeeding twins is difficult to do subtly. Whatever modesty issues I may have had at the beginning quickly disappeared as it is truly impossible to be discreet when tandem nursing. The good news, of course, is that there is so much baby hanging out all over you that there is really nothing left to see! I never expected to nurse in front of as many people as I did. The thing is, though, that we lived in a small apartment- there was one place to nurse and it was in the living room where any visitors also were. I say this first because I think it's important to understand: people were much less uncomfortable than I expected them to be; the visitors and myself included. Once you are practiced with getting the babies to latch, the nursing part itself is easy to conceal. The nursing pillow will cover your stomach, your shirt can rest gently on the babies heads and you will be fully covered by babies.

One of the wonderful parts of breastfeeding, that special time between you and your babies, is also a part that is difficult for some to understand. Others who wish so much to help will offer to give a baby a bottle and will want to give you a rest. When your hormones are in flux and so much of the day feels hard, nursing can give you a short period of respite from it all. Rather than feeling obliged to sit in one place, nursing can be a time of peace and relaxation. Your babies are happy and quiet except for the little noises they make while sucking. You can breathe deeply and enjoy the moments where there is nothing else for you to do. It is a wonderful experience, and it is difficult to explain to others who have not experienced it. Resistance from others may come because they did not breastfeed themselves or maybe they don't know what else to offer to do. Your best bet is to appreciate what they are trying to do for you and offer them another way to help. "Thank you for offering to feed one of the babies but this works really well for us. I wonder if you could [change the crib sheets, throw in a load of laundry, prepare a snack for me, take the dog for a walk, etc]."

The Hard Days

Breastfeeding is not easy, especially in the beginning. Your body and your psyche need time to adjust. It took several weeks before I could even feel the let down (it feels like pins and needles if you're wondering what to look for). It took time to be able to control how much leakage I had when I was not nursing, and soreness was sometimes overwhelming. It was difficult to figure out how to juggle timing and I always had to be ready for someone to be hungry. It is easy for fatigue to overwhelm any bit of patience and motivation you might have available for what can certainly feel like a chore.

The very hardest days, however, involved growth spurts. You do not necessarily know you are in the middle of a growth spurt until you find yourself tearing out your hair and wondering why someone is always hungry and you are certain they just ate! You might feel empty and someone, or two, is still hungry. The crying begins, your patience wanes, and you just want to throw your own little temper tantrum about being tired of nursing.

Getting through these difficult days of physical and psychological strain can be done. I developed my own little mantra- "I will nurse just for today." Somehow, getting up each morning and declaring that I would make breastfeeding work today (only) made it seem more manageable. The choice was mine and I would choose to make it work for this day. Looking ahead a few hours was much easier than looking ahead by days and weeks, especially when each hour felt so challenging. Knowing what you want makes it much easier to work towards. Once you are psychologically poised to make the day work, problem solving for the physical and logistical can be done.

When your body is challenged the way it is when you are nursing, you must know what tools to use to help it recover. I used three main treatments to help my skin breakdown and nipple soreness. First, breast milk itself has healing properties and after nursing it is advised that you rub a little bit of the excess milk around the nipple itself and let it air dry a few moments. Second, I used Lansinoh cream after every nursing session when my skin was in bad shape. You will want to check and make sure that the cream you use does not have to be washed off prior to nursing- I generally did anyways, but I did not want to not have to worry about whatever cream I used being harmful to my babies. Recommendations differ by brand of cream. Finally, gel packs, frequently sold labeled as disposable, that are kept in the freezer and used inside the bra in between feedings were my savior in those early weeks. I used and reused the packs I had despite their directions, as they are expensive! They worked very well for me and provided much needed relief in between feedings. The key thing to remember is to get them back into the freezer when you are going to start nursing so that they are ready for you when you are done!

Breastfeeding While Out

There is perhaps no harder time to be a nursing mother of twins than when you are not at home and both babies need to eat. The truth is that most nursing mothers of twins stay very close to home most of the time in the first months. Or, they plan their trips out immediately following a nursing session and know that they likely only have one to one and a half hours before they need to be home to feed someone again. When I say immediately following, I mean, literally, walk out the door when you are done. All of the diaper bag preparations, getting yourself ready, locating your purse, keys and phone must be done before you start nursing. You may even have the car loaded with this gear before you begin feeding! Every minute counts- I promise.

Assuming that you make it out of the house with both babies, unless you are in a friendly environment with your twin nursing pillow, it will be virtually impossible to tandem feed. If you are visiting someone who is understanding of your situation, by all means, do not be embarrassed to throw your pillow in the car. While it can sometimes be overwhelming to travel with as much stuff as is required for newborn (x2) care, your nursing pillow should be seen as essential equipment. Your back will thank you later for providing appropriate support! If you are more comfortable, excuse yourself to another room when you feed your babies while not at home.

If you are not at home and you are either in a place where you are unprepared to nurse or it is not possible to tandem feed, like malls or doctor's offices, for example, you will need a different strategy. First, it must be said that feeding will not go smoothly all of the time. Sometimes one baby will have to nurse first and the other will have to wait- they will cry and there is nothing you can do about it. I have tried pushing and pulling the stroller back and forth with my feet while they are in it. I have tried rocking the car seat up and down with my foot. I have tried pacifiers and I have tried holding both babies myself, or having someone else hold one, while I feed the other. There is no perfect system and any one of these methods might work (or not) on any given day.

The best chance you have for smooth sequential feedings comes if you can feed the first baby before they realize they are hungry. Watch the clock, know how often both babies generally feed, and feed the first baby about ten minutes ahead of their average schedule. The idea is to catch the first baby before they feel hungry, so that they are close to done when the second baby gets hungry. Who you feed first, in this situation, depends on a number of factors. Perhaps one baby is always hungry first- feed them. Perhaps one baby didn't eat as much at the last feeding- feed them. Perhaps one baby is faster than the other at eating- feed them. Perhaps one baby will take the pacifier- feed the one who will not. Perhaps one is sound asleep- feed the one who is awake. You will get practiced at making these decisions and patterns may or may not emerge that will help you make future decisions.

Never be afraid to try a new system and do not be afraid to see what works and doesn't work. Know that if all else fails you can leave wherever you are and find a place to tandem nurse. I have nursed in the front and back seats of my caravan. In fact, one of our best nursing stories is stopping in a random company's parking lot about a half hour from our destination to tandem feed both kids when everything fell apart driving in the car. It was dark, it was raining, and my husband crawled into the back of the car to hand the babies up to me in the front seat. Some moms think to always throw their nursing pillow in the car so that it is available to them even if they never plan to use it!

When You Need Help

No matter how experienced you are with nursing, nursing twins is a whole new world. It is very likely that on one occasion or another you will benefit from everything from friendly advice to professional coaching. For those who have never nursed a baby before, as was my situation, you are learning both how to nurse and how to nurse twins at the same time. You need general advice (like how to unclog a duct or what to do if you're so full that it is hard for the babies to latch) and you need the twin-specific advice (like how to hold them so you can tandem nurse or how to do anything else during the day besides nurse babies).

Advice is plentiful, but knowing where to look and who to ask when you need it is critical. Most important is to find outlets you trust and go to them when you need to. You will likely encounter plenty of unsolicited advice from others who do not understand your desire to succeed. Maybe they did not nurse their children or maybe they can't imagine that one mother could make enough milk to feed two babies. Once you identify someone as unsupportive, avoid all discussions with them about nursing. It is very important for you to have supporters and fans. It is too exhausting to have to explain yourself and your decision-making to others.

Your community may have many resources available to you at no charge. La Leche League is a wonderful resource available to parents. Local chapters frequently run groups that you can attend with your babies to receive help, guidance, and reassurance. You can actually attend some of these groups, as I did, while pregnant to gain a better understanding of what you need to know. The truth is that after my babies were born I truly could not see a way to get them out of the house and to a meeting, despite the help that would be available when I arrived. At the time, La Leche League held online meetings as well. They had a calendar, which I printed and posted, of daily live chat sessions. You could log-in to these meetings at a certain time each day and get help in live time. I did this frequently in the early days when I was trying to figure everything out, and, later on, when I needed help with a specific issue.

When my babies were first born I was not well-connected to my local "Parents of Twins" group. Becoming connected later on, however, and being a member ever since, I can say with great certainty that this group would be an invaluable resource for any nursing mother. These mothers have nursed multiples successfully and have run into every problem you can think of already. They have tips and tricks, they have supportive words, and they'll give you their phone number- so you can call them when you think you can't do it anymore. They might stop by with a coffee, and they might send you an email out of the blue- on just the day you think you've had it. Connecting with other mothers who are currently nursing and those who have successfully nursed is an amazing opportunity to solidify your own expectations. If you want to nurse, and you see that others have done it, maybe you can do it too.

If you have the resources to pay for professional help, lactation consultants and postpartum doulas may be helpful. The hospital, your local "Parents of Twins" Group, and La Leche League may be able to recommend specific providers who have experience working with mothers of twins. These professionals may be able to come to your home and help you evaluate how you are doing- whether there are technique issues or whether your baby has physical issues (with their tongue or neck) that are causing difficulty. While an investment, if breastfeeding is important to you and you are struggling, it is money well-spent. Remember, the cost of formula for two adds up quickly as well!

When Breastfeeding Gets Easy

So much about breastfeeding has to do with getting it right in the beginning. It is, I guess, a little bit like riding a bike. Once you get it, it doesn't go away. The good news about this is that each day you and your babies can improve, and those gains will stay! What this also means is that there will be a point at which you realize that nursing has become second nature. This is a wonderful moment and you should be sure to celebrate all that you have accomplished. Suddenly, all of the "hard" that you have been through becomes worthwhile. There are no bottles to wash and no formula to mix. You don't have to listen to your babies cry while you heat up their milk. The payback is worth it and you can enjoy the months of "easy" that you have ahead of you.

There will still be hard days here and there- when the babies hit growth spurts or when the babies begin teething, and don't want to nurse because of sore and painful gums. Here and there you'll still run into challenges. But overall, nursing will become a time you can relax and enjoy- a "magic bullet" we used to call it, for grumpy babies who needed to be "re-set." No matter how and when you start, it is likely that by twelve weeks you will find that you are an accomplished nursing mother. Hang in there and know you can do it.

Nursing as they Grow

The first twelve months of a baby's life brings so many changes. Everything about nursing, it seems, can change from the beginning of those months to the end. Your babies will get bigger, and longer, and heavier. They start out so small on the nursing pillow and sometime along the way you find that their feet are touching the back of the couch. They are so light you can carry them all over the house on the nursing pillow, and then suddenly you find your knees no longer hold them up with out extra pillows underneath to take some of the weight. Your babies are growing. They are getting distracted by noises and people in your home. They try to crane their head around to see what is behind them without letting go of their latch- ouch!

How you nurse them as they grow is completely dependent on what is comfortable for you. As they got bigger, the nursing pillow became less helpful and I generally found it comfortable to sit in the glider in their room with both babies one on each leg, facing each other. The chair reclined a bit and we all leaned back and in. They were essentially sitting, facing each other, looking up towards me to nurse. I continued nursing my babies several times a day- in the morning when they woke, prior to naps and before bed for as long as they were interested for about ten or eleven months. As they became less interested, I started to cut back.

Weaning

When they begin eating more solid foods and nursing becomes less consistent, perhaps you begin thinking about weaning, and about being tired of nursing- feeling like you've given your babies a strong start with what you have done. Unless you have a target date- like six months, or the babies first birthday, you might wonder how you decide when you are going to stop.

Before I got pregnant with twins, I always imagined I would nurse my baby until they were one-year-old and were ready to switch to cow's milk. As difficult as nursing was in the beginning, I kept up my "I will only nurse today" mantra for a long time. Once I reached the point where nursing was "easy," I decided I could do it until the babies switched to cow's milk. I targeted one year from my babies' 40 week due date. Due to some initial sensitivities my son had to dairy due to an "immature gut," I decided to wait until he was one, adjusted age, before trying cow's milk. Looking at the calendar, however, and seeing our first plane flight scheduled about a month later, we decided that having the "magic bullet" handy would be a good thing and my goal was to keep nursing until after that trip. I was getting tired, though, and began anticipating the weaning process around eleven months or so. In the end, my twins nursed until they were one week shy of fifteen months old. It was the right time for us and I am very proud of what I did.

Something I found surprising was how hard it was, physically, to wean. After working so hard to build up a solid and reliable milk supply, slowing down the milk production machine was a bit more challenging than I expected! In order to not be engorged, whenever I thought about dropping a feeding I tried first to shorten the feeding. I tried to have the babies stop nursing a little bit shy of when they might usually, so that I didn't empty every time. Again, this was harder than I anticipated and I had to adjust my expectations about how long it would take to cut out a feeding. For my own comfort this went very slowly. From the time they turned one, their official birthday, until the time we officially weaned, I slowly started shortening feedings.

I will never forget the true end of nursing. It was a Friday night when I thought I was done nursing. I nursed my babies to sleep and thought that I was done. It was bittersweet; as much as I was tired and was ready to be relieved of the responsibility, I also knew that it was the end of a special time in all of our lives. I did not nurse them the whole weekend, and, though I felt very full and not very comfortable, I was doing okay. By Monday morning I woke up so engorged and in so much pain, I told my husband "I have nursed those babies for almost 15 months whenever they needed to... today they are nursing for me!" I had my husband go get the babies, and I had them nurse off some of the milk so I wasn't in quite so much pain. And, that was the last time I nursed them. My milk production gradually stopped and the babies didn't miss nursing. It was the right time for them as well.

PUMPING

What Kind of Pump

If you come home from the hospital pumping, or you need to pump in order to go back to work you will want to consider a few things. The kind of pump you use can have a large impact on your success. If you are coming home from the hospital without your babies, I highly recommend renting a hospital grade pump, at least initially. The hospital will likely help set you up with this rental upon discharge and I cannot overstate how different these pumps are from the personal, home pumps that many women purchase. If you are exclusively pumping, and trying to establish your supply without the benefit of the most-efficient, nursing babies, you will appreciate the efficiency of the hospital-grade pump. Some health insurance policies cover the rental of this pump (or the purchase of a personal pump) depending on your plan and circumstances. Contact your insurance company's customer service line to verify pump coverage prior to your babies birth if you are able. Once your milk supply is well-established, perhaps after the first month or so, a double, individual electric pump can work fine, though you will notice the difference if you were using a hospital-grade pump prior.

If you do begin pumping while your babies are in the hospital, the hospital may provide a "pump kit-" essentially all parts that touch the milk that are required to hook up to the brand of pumps available in the hospital. These kits can later be hooked up to the individual electric pumps, allowing you to purchase a pump machine second-hand or borrow from a friend. The "pump kit" itself is not inexpensive and deciding to switch brands to a pump compatible with the kit you have after discharge should be considered even if you have previously picked out a different pump.

Pumping Successfully

In addition to how efficient the pump is, how many ounces of milk you are able to pump will be affected by your ability to relax and get a good let-down. It really is more of a "mind game" than you might imagine! For new mothers who may be stressed by a range of circumstances- everything from adjusting to new babies at home to very sick babies still in the hospital- it can be difficult to relax enough to pump successfully. I suggest, if you can, that you pump alone. Go to a quiet room, set everything up, take some deep breaths and try to calm yourself. You need to put your mind in a quiet and peaceful state. You can do this in many ways. In the beginning, when my babies were in the NICU and I was home without them, a little photo book with pictures of them accompanied me everywhere. I found that looking at their pictures while trying to relax prior to pumping increased my success. Later on, when the babies were home, I sometimes tried to read and let my mind escape. Learning to make your body relax and "let-down" while pumping increases your chances of keeping your milk supply in line with what the babies need.

Milk Storage

You will also want to consider milk storage after pumping. When my babies were in the NICU, the hospital provided bags full of pumping supplies so that I could pump right into little bottles that would then be used for feeding. Each night I would take home a new pump kit, fill the bottles all night, and bring back the milk for storage for my babies at the hospital each day. Initially I was producing milk about as fast as my babies were using it- at the beginning they were tube fed my breast milk. As my milk production got ahead of my babies, I began to freeze it so that I had some stored for the future. I banked quite a bit of milk while my babies were in the NICU, and this was very helpful later on. You will have to determine how much freezer space you have, what type of storage will be easiest, and how you will be using the milk. For example, will you be transferring it to bottles or inserting bagged milk into bottles designed for such purposes. If you have the choice, pumping right into whatever storage container you will ultimately be using to feed is, by far, the easiest.

BOTTLE FEEDING

Whether you are bottle-feeding pumped milk or formula you will likely want to try out a number of different strategies right away in order to figure out what makes the process work the best. Like all parts of baby-care, what works, or doesn't for you will be different than for other families. That being said, hearing advice and ideas from many different people will allow you to select the most reasonable options for you.

What Kind and How Much

First, you will want to consider what you're feeding the baby and how much with the advice of your babies' physician. If you are not bottle-feeding breast milk, you will want to specifically discuss your formula options with the doctors prior to discharge from the hospital. There are all kinds of formula and what you choose may or may not be important based on your babies' situation at birth. Make sure you ask what they recommend and why. Also ask (especially if it's a specific formulation) how long this particular kind will be recommended (so that you can purchase the right amount- no more, no less!). You may want to ask if you can switch brands once your baby is established on one- perhaps because you were given some free samples, or because you've found a source for a less expensive kind. Your babies' physician should be your guide for all decisions about what kind of formula and how much to feed them.

Logistics

With regard to how to feed them and how to make double-bottle-feeding work, your best source of support are the mothers who have done it before you. Sometimes, the smallest of details will actually make a significant difference in the level of difficulty of a task! I have a friend who kept a little dorm-sized refrigerator in the babies room, so that there were always bottles ready throughout the night. Another friend kept a crockpot full of water on low, so that there was always a place ready to warm up bottles. Some families like to mix up a day's worth of formula in a large pitcher, others measure it out by the bottle.

Bottle feeding two babies is twice as challenging as bottle-feeding one! This is a good time to share your babies love with whomever is around to help you feed one. Enjoy the time you have with a single baby and make the minutes count. Don't worry about not feeding both babies at any given feeding. When you are on your own, some parents will prop their babies up in Boppy-style pillows so that they can hold bottles with both hands. Others use a towel or other specifically-designed bottle prop in order to make sure that both babies are able to eat when they are hungry. You will need to figure out a system that works for you and your family- for everything from anticipating hunger and having bottles ready when you want them, to burping and bottle-feeding two babies at the same time. My only caution is to remember that feeding is a task which happens over and over each day. Each and every experience does not have to be memory-making. You should never feel guilty for using extra "hands," whether those are living hands of another person, or pillows or props. Sometimes, the babies are just hungry and feeding both, at the same time, while either the bottles or the babies are propped is just a method for getting your babies what they need. Advice about bottle-feeding one baby, truly cannot be applied to feeding two.

INFANT FEEDING SUMMARY

Feeding infants is tricky. No matter how you do it, the tasks, patience, and attentiveness required for feeding multiple infants is significant. Making sure your babies get the amount of milk or formula they need each day is truly the most important job you have. Remember that there are lots of ways to show love and lots of ways to spend time with your babies. Whether you nurse, or do not; whether you are available for every feeding, or are not; or whether you find yourself just as disorganized a few weeks in as you were the very first day they came home does not matter. Ask for help- from your babies' doctor, from friends, from neighbors- if you need it. If you have the resources, hire help to help you get on the right track. Remember that there is no right way to do any of this, there are just ways that work better or worse for each family at any given point in the babies' lives.

11 JOURNAL: NOV 2ND, 6TH

Wednesday, November 2nd

Well, the adventures here continue. The twins are now 7 and a half weeks old and there haven't been many days over this time period where we haven't been totally stressed out!

We ended up in the Pediatric ER on Saturday afternoon as Owen was screaming and inconsolable (a new scream, not just the I'm not happy scream), hadn't been eating (which, as I've said before, you can pretty much set the clock by him), screamed when you moved him, was lethargic... all in all, not himself. After a couple hours of making sure we'd tried everything we knew, we decided something wasn't right and we should take him in to be seen.

To make a long story short, he ended up being admitted to the hospital (in the wee hours of Sunday morning, actually) and underwent surgery for repair of an incarcerated inguinal hernia on Monday morning. Essentially, all of this was a complication of prematurity. He was in a lot of pain.

So, in the ER the surgeons managed to push everything back into the right place manually (after sedating Owen). They wanted to wait a day to do surgery to close everything back up after the swelling had gone down a bit. When doing the surgery, they took a little camera to check the other side and saw that the same problem was there (though it hadn't manifested itself yet)...so they fixed that too.

Owen was discharged from the hospital yesterday (Tuesday) and we are all glad to be together at home again. Owen was a real trooper... I mean, how doing you tell a 7 week old he can't eat for a certain number of hours before surgery!

Mom and dad are thinking this parenting thing is ridiculously hard and are waiting for the fun part! The amount of medical nonsense we've had to deal with in their short life is incredible! On top of that, it's a logistical nightmare to have twins...with only one admitted to the hospital (especially when breastfeeding)! Mike ended up staying with Owen the first night, and I took Charlotte home. Then I stayed with Owen the 2nd and 3rd nights and Mike took Charlotte home. Add in, trying to pump milk (when one kid wasn't eating), get some sleep in a semi-private room with 2 infants (who of course don't sleep at the same time), and stay in a 4x9ft space with two babies, one of whom is feeling just "fine"... And, well, it was a little stressful. :)

We're all glad to be home. Owen is feeling much better. Periodic freak-outs at this point, mostly when he is waking up, and probably trying to figure out if he's still in the hospital or not! Charlotte, of course, also could sense something was wrong and both babies are getting a little extra sleep today- we're all exhausted!

Sunday, November 6th

We're 8 weeks old now... and getting bigger by the day! Still no regular patterns to our day- we like to eat and sleep at all hours. We do enjoy being up in the middle of the night, though mom is solving that problem by just taking us to bed with her. She has an easier time ignoring us when we're right next to her and she knows we're okay. Don't think that that means we're cooperative! We do our best to get her to play... sometimes though, she's just cranky in the middle of the night! She should really take more naps! :)

We're having fun and are excited to start meeting all of mom & dad's friends now that we're a little bigger and stronger! See you soon!

Love, Owen and Charlotte

12 WHEN THINGS GO WRONG

At some point in your babies lives, though hopefully never, of course, something might "go wrong." Someone might get sick, or fall, or get hurt in some other way. I wish I could say that the chances of this happening were low, but I can't. Instead I can say with certainty that knowing in advance how you will handle it will make whatever the scenario go far more smoothly. Despite my background as a medical social worker, and my experience helping countless families in similar situations, when my son went to the emergency room the very first time, we were definitely not prepared. Here is the information I believe every parent should think through at least once when they have babies so that they are prepared for all eventualities.

Getting Care

First, know what hospital your family will use. Identify both the closest hospital to you, in the event of a serious emergency, and the hospital you might prefer to go to-because that is where your doctor is affiliated, because that is where there is a designated pediatric department, or because that is the hospital that participates with your insurance carrier. In the event of a serious emergency you will want to go to the closest hospital and that hospital will stabilize your child before helping them get care at the most appropriate place.

Second, if your child is sick, you should be in contact with their doctor, or the covering physician after hours, in order to have them help you determine the best course of care. Know what your insurance carrier requires in terms of getting a prior authorization for care. Obviously, in the event of a life-threatening emergency you would call your community emergency response system- 911, or whatever system is in place in your location. If you are already in contact with your child's physician, however, and their physician refers you to the hospital, it can make billing matters proceed more smoothly.

Third, make sure all of your health insurance information is in your wallet. You will want to have access to your contract and group numbers as well as the insurance customer service number while you are out getting your child care. While you may not wish to think about certain matters like whether an ambulance transport between hospitals is a covered benefit or a certain pharmacy accepts your insurance coverage, I promise that three weeks later you will. If you are overwhelmed by everything that is happening, you can ask for help sorting through this information at the hospital itself- they generally have patient account representatives or social workers available to assist families. You must have your coverage information with you, though. Do yourself a favor and put a card in your wallet and keep it there. You now have children.

Obviously in the event of serious and immediate emergency you will have limited, if any, time to think. Many times, though, even for urgent trips to the emergency room, you will have a few minutes to pull together the most necessary supplies. Unfortunately, I can tell you from experience that you get better at both anticipating when things are going downhill, and prepping for that occasion quickly. Remember, even if you can't get your belongings organized and into a bag, throwing them in the car so that they are accessible at the hospital when matters have calmed down a little bit is helpful.

One of my biggest fears as a parent of twins was having an emergency and needing to care for two babies. Our first trip to the emergency room, and subsequent admission and surgery taught me that it was both a well-founded fear and that being better prepared would have been helpful. Here are the things I either forgot to bring or should have brought with me to the emergency room.

Cell phone, keys and wallet (with cash)-

Extra handy if you bring or keep a cell phone charger in the car. Sure this might seem like an "of course" list, but it is hard to call family for help or to let them know how things are going if you don't have your phone. It is hard to use the pay phone when you forget your cell phone if you don't have cash or coins. It is hard to purchase any food from the cafeteria without cash. And your keys, don't forget that you might hand them over to the valets when you pull up to emergency. It's okay if you can't find them once you're at the hospital.

Diaper Bags-

It is helpful to have at least one, if not both diaper bags available to you. If they were both packed and ready this will assure you have supplies for basic baby care available to you while you figure out what is going on and how you are going to manage going forward. It is especially nice to have a few snacks for mom and dad available in these diaper bags should you, at some point, realize you haven't eaten in hours.

Breast Pump-

If you are nursing and have a breast pump, it is helpful to throw it in the car along with some cold packs in an insulated cooler. Even if your babies normally breast feed and do not bottle feed, if one baby either does not wish to feed or cannot for medical reasons, you will want to pump their portion. This is important for your comfort and so that the milk is available later on if and when they're ready to eat and you either are not available or they're super hungry and your supply isn't quite where it needs to be due to the stress. You might imagine that something like a breast pump would be easy to find in a hospital, but the pump kits are expensive, the pumping rooms are likely located within the inpatient floors and not in the emergency department, and you will want to be by your child's side for however many hours you are in emergency. Having your own pump, to use at your baby's bedside, is easiest.

Personal Items-

If you have time, throw together a little overnight bag with some comfortable clothes, a toothbrush, hairbrush and hair band, glasses or contact solution, and maybe a book or personal electronic gadget for the middle of the night when you're wide awake and can't sleep. I have put this little kit together on more than one occasion, in preparation for any eventuality, after I learned how helpful it would have been that first trip to the hospital.

Managing Twins When One is Hospitalized

I have friends with far too much more practice in this area of twin parenting. I am so fortunate to have had only one experience with the matter. Having your babies physically in two different locations, and more so having one with medical needs is extremely taxing on the parents. You will necessarily need multiple adults to shuttle people and babies around. If the hospital allows your second infant to spend time at the hospital this will make some things easier, but the truth is that managing two babies in the hospital is no picnic.

You will want to consider who stays in the hospital with the admitted baby and who takes the other home at night. You might switch off, trying to see what makes the most sense. When my son was hospitalized and I was breastfeeding, the first night I took my daughter home. I ended up being up to breastfeed, followed by pumping for my son, almost the entire night. The next night I stayed at the hospital and pumped for both babies at once, saving myself a little bit of time, allowing me to sleep a few hours. Hospital sleep, though, if you don't already know, is not good sleep, so whomever stays there will likely be running on very little sleep regardless.

Longer term child care planning is virtually impossible in a hospital setting so do not plan on having a schedule. From day to day or hour to hour you will likely not know how much longer your child will be admitted. So much depends on the treatment plan and how your baby responds to it. Ongoing dialogue with the medical team can help you feel comfortable with what is happening and what needs to happen before your baby is discharged. If you are ever confused or unsure about the plan, ask the hospital staff for help. Doctors, nurses, and social workers are available to help you understand what is happening and can help you think through plans for your non-admitted baby during this time.

How Others Can Help

If you have other family and friends who live nearby and are offering to help, here are some things they can do. When they ask, don't be shy- give them this list.

Bring you meals-
Bring meals both to your house for whomever takes one child home at night and to the hospital so that you an have a decent, homemade meal to eat while you are there. Extra frozen meals in the freezer for when you get home are also helpful. Your baby will likely have a difficult time transitioning back home and your days will be very full helping them feel at ease.

Clean your house-
It's likely that you walked out of the house in whatever state it was when you realized there was a problem. Maybe there are still dinner dishes on the table or food sitting out, and maybe there are mountains of laundry. Don't be shy, let people help you. When your baby is ready to come home they will need lots of extra care and you will not likely not have time to do the regular chores, let alone "catch up" with the build up, when you do.

Pick Up "Necessities"-

Comfort foods, candy, a hot drink, lip gloss, hand lotion, soft tissues, silly magazines- let friends drop them by the hospital for you.

Lend an Ear-

Let friends visit the hospital (if allowed) or call to check on you, send you an email, and help you communicate news with friends. Understanding and coping with medical issues is challenging, stressful, and scary. A friendly face or a caring voice can help you reduce some of your tension and give you the strength to get through the next few hours.

Returning Home

Whenever your baby is discharged from the hospital you will likely feel both relief and perhaps a bit of fear. Knowing you have professionals caring for your baby while they are admitted is very reassuring, and depending on the reason for admission, you may have some anxiety about being the one to monitor your little one again at home. You will come home with complete discharge instructions- letting you know how to best care for your baby and when to call or bring the baby in for help. You will likely have a follow-up visit scheduled with your baby's doctor within a few days to a week's time. In the meantime, know that you can always call your baby's doctor with any questions or if you need help understanding the discharge instructions.

Know that both you and your baby have been through a traumatic time and it will likely take some time for your baby to adjust again to life at home. Just as you found when you first brought your baby home, if they were admitted for a longer stay at birth, the sights, sounds, and lighting are all different at home. Your baby has been through a lot and may not want to be put down without protest. They may wake in the middle of the night and not return to sleep without comfort, even if they did prior to the admission. Give your baby, and yourself time to adjust to being home again before your expectations return. Know that it's normal for fear you may have held back during the admission to come charging out now that you're home and you know your baby is okay. Trouble sleeping, conflicting moods, and more general feelings of overwhelm are normal and common. These should dissipate gradually as life returns to normal. If you feel as though you or your baby are continuing to have trouble, seek the advice of a physician.

13 JOURNAL: DEC 3RD, 31ST

Saturday, December 3rd

Well, this last month has just flown by. I kept meaning to update the website and, well, never had half a second to do it! So, here are some ramblings about what's going on now.

Tonight Mike is on-call; spending the night at the hospital. Last night was his first overnight since the twins were born. He had a good night- got about as much sleep as he usually does here at home with us. :) Owen is currently stirring, he's supposed to be napping in the pack and play, listening to Barbara Streisand's Christmas CD by the light of the Christmas tree. Charlotte is asleep in the Baby Bjorn (a soft, front carrier that I wear). She loves it cause she can snuggle right up to me, and I love it, cause it allows both my hands to be free while she's happy. :)

The past month has been fast and furious. The babies are putting on weight like crazy, which I only know to be true because my back, neck, knees, and arms complain every night when I lay down. With every day, though, we are rewarded with visible development. Most fun, are the smiles that have appeared. They have just recently begun smiling reflexively- if they're in the right mood, when we smile at them, they'll smile back. Their best time of day is the first hour after they wake up in the morning. They're just so happy, they love to look at the light coming in the windows, particularly that which comes in between the slats of the vertical blinds. And, wow do we get some great smiles at that time of day!

While the babies are 12 weeks old chronologically, at this point their age is still "adjusted" for prematurity. Essentially what this means is that we can't expect them to be acting like a true 12 week old. They'll catch up quickly to their full-term peers, but we have to keep their adjusted age (6.5 weeks) in mind when looking at how they're doing. The main area where this comes into play is sleep. As in, I'd like more of it, for longer stretches. :) We've had 3 nights total when I've been able to get 4 hours uninterrupted. Most nights, I continue to get 1-2 hours at a time.

We could, really, do a sitcom of the overnight happenings. Charlotte is ridiculously difficult to get to bed. She has to be completely OUT before you put her down, or her eyelids fly open, her face scrunches up, and she lets out a scream like "how could you DO this to me." As you can imagine, this little monologue has a high potential to interrupt Owen. However, if you don't put Owen down first, he will definitely disturb Charlotte, who is also a very light sleeper. Now, let's say you actually get them both down (which took me 1 hour and 45 minutes last night without Mike- had to feed them both again during the process cause it took so long!)- the rest of the night is just as tentative. Owen likes to eat frequently, but he will wake up, eat, and go back to sleep, or will lay in his crib quietly with his eyes open- no problem. Charlotte, however...refer to above about getting her back to sleep. And the thing is, you want to wake her to eat when Owen does, so that you're not up every hour feeding one of them. It is often the case, though, that you are up for the entire two hours between when Owen likes to eat just getting Charlotte back to bed. The other night I actually fell asleep in the rocker holding her. I got up to feed them at 11:30, put Owen to bed, and then tried to rock Charlotte to sleep. Next thing I know, it's 2am and Owen's ready to eat again... :) We continue to experiment with various combinations of napping patterns through the day, and waking patterns at night to see if anything works better. (The funniest part of that last sentence is the word "patterns," cause there really are none- but if a night goes better we say to ourselves, "oh, maybe it was because they slept at such and such a time, or were up for this much time.") :)

Saturday, December 31, 2005

Well 2005 has sure been a whirlwind year! I'm looking forward to 2006 and am hoping that some semblance of a "normal" schedule begins to appear. :) I know that I'm wishing for something that's sure to be impossible with twins, but hey, there's no use in dwelling on that. We're definitely in a "reach for the stars" mindset around here.

For example, last night I only got up one time to feed our little critters :). Fed them at 10:30, went to bed, Owen woke up around 3am, so I got Owen up and woke Charlotte (only enough for her to eat), then everyone went back to bed.

Actually, Owen didn't fall back asleep, but as he was content to lay in his crib and look at his bumper pad and mobile, I was content to let him and return to bed myself. :) Didn't wake up again until 7:30am when Charlotte decided to make her presence known. I again woke the sleeping twin, only to find that Charlotte really wasn't very hungry, but just ready to get up and play. :) So that we did, for an hour, till we decided that dad was missing too much fun and we should really get him up too. :) For that, I'm sure he will be eternally grateful. :)

We're having a quiet New Years Eve this year. We just returned from spending Christmas in Ohio with Mike's family. The babies took their first long car trip and did, well, ok for part of the time...the rest of the time...they screamed. :) So, after lots of visitors and travel we're all content to be homebound and relaxed today. The babies are actually asleep at the same time right now. Though I can hear some stirrings from time to time... almost lunchtime apparently. :)

Christmas was fun. The babies, of course, had no concept of anything, but did enjoy the attention lavished upon them. They got some toys which they are enjoying and they're beginning to engage with the world around them which is fun to watch. With this fun, however, comes some downsides. Now, if one of them is crying and the other isn't sure we are appropriately concerned, they will chime in to insure that we are aware there is a problem... :)

Charlotte got her first virus this week- boy that was fun...lots of screaming, fussing, and a nice rash to show off. Don't think we've gotten rid of it quite yet. Owen so far as managed to avoid the bug, but we'll see if that lasts.

Despite not feeling well, Charlotte rolled over (front to back) for the first time last week! It was very exciting- she managed a few repeat performances later that day, but she hasn't been interested in doing it since!

So...as 2005 comes to a close I'm happy to say we're ready to tackle 2006. :) Happy New Year!

14 THE HEAD GAME

Being pregnant invites advice and stories of all kinds, from all kinds, and at all times. Sometimes this advice is well-timed, as in "that's the stroller my daughter has; she likes it a lot" while you're at the baby superstore evaluating options for double-strollers that will hold up like the Conestoga wagons of yesteryear. Sometimes what someone thinks is advice is actually a story in disguise, meant to signify that the person knows what you're going through whether they do or not, as in, "my friend was on bed-rest for three months when she was pregnant with her twins." Sometimes the advice comes from professionals, like your physician, when they recommend "getting as much help as possible after the babies arrive." All of these types of advice and the countless others that make their way through your brain during pregnancy likely did little to help your psyche unless they were confirming something you thought you knew or wanted to be true. Every other kind expression and flippant comment very well could have caused you to rethink all you knew on a particular subject.

Unfortunately, for me, this did not stop after the babies were born. I have found nothing about parenting that is easy or straightforward and I have found few things harder than what I have called "the head game." Overall what this refers to is keeping your expectations and comparisons in check. Sometimes this means catching yourself in a panic when referring to the "what to expect" checklists of developmental tasks. Sometimes this means being careful when comparing your child to that of your best friend, playgroup companions, and child in the next cart at the grocery store. Sometimes this means boosting your own psyche when you're convinced that you are not able to be the parent you want to be. These are problems that I am sure are faced by every parent all of the time. I would argue, however, that parents of twins are predisposed to be challenged more deeply on more of these issues.

Being Enough

One of the most significant areas of self-doubt for twin parents is that of "being enough." With two unique individuals depending on you for everything, from the very beginning you feel torn. You want to shower all of your love and care on your baby so that they feel every morsel of your effort- and yet you have two to do this for. Try as you might, most parents of twins I know have, on many occasions, felt as though they have shorted their babies. If you are giving your all, each baby must be getting only half of it and how can that be enough? When one baby cries and your arms are full with another, when one baby is hospitalized and the other is home, when one baby lays for an extra few minutes with a dirty diaper because *this time* you picked up the other baby to change them first- how can you not feel conflicted?

There is no easy answer for this feeling and it is one that you will likely struggle with as your children grow. You might hope that as they get older the feeling will be less, but it really will not. At the preschool ice cream social one child may want you to hold their hand in the background, taking in all the activity. The other child may want you to help them run and play with new friends. This feeling is one that you must learn to control and navigate in your own mind- there is just no physical fix for it. Even with a second adult, even with your spouse, when you are focused on one child you will feel as though you are not focused on the other.

As you grow in your parent-of-twins role, your ability to manage these inherent conflicts will improve even though it does not feel like it ever could. To get started on this process, remember a few points. First, simple math will never work when it comes to what parents give their children. Parents can give 100% to two children and it does not mean that each child will receive 50% of the whole. Just as they say in survey results, the sum of the percentages may not add up to 100%.

Second, we have taught our children that in our house, "fair" means making sure that each person has what they need, not that everything is always the same. You will find that there are weeks, months, even years that pass where one child will seemingly need more from you than the other. You will feel like you are short-changing the child who is doing well and you will feel like you are "missing" out on the fun while your focus is directed on the one who is struggling more at the moment. But time will turn and needs will change and you will look back and realize that your children have really shared you better than you thought. I can count by years when saying which child struggled more or needed me more, but they both have had me when they needed me. That is, as a parent, what you do.

Finally, you have heard the adage "misery loves company." I remember a cartoon in my undergraduate psychology textbook where a man and a women who lived in neighboring apartment buildings looked across their balconies at each other. One said to the other "do you really love me, or is just because I live on the 21st floor." The lesson from that cartoon is that people who are struggling don't just need others' company, they need others struggling with the same issues that they are. Finding an outlet for your worries, fears, and struggles as a parent of twins will provide you with peace of mind that you may not have realized that you needed. Finding other parents of twins to gain ideas and support from-either online or through local parents of twins groups- can offer you a mirror into your own world. It is a place where you can learn from others who have successfully navigated stages you have yet to enter. It is a place where you can share what worked (or didn't) for you, and in doing so, be reminded of how far you have come. Parents who start these friendships with other parents of twins when they are pregnant have someone they know from the very beginning, who can support them through all of the crazy and hard that comes full speed ahead when those babies are born.

Adjusted Age

My babies were born at 34 weeks and 4 days. This meant they were born approximately five and a half weeks earlier than a standard forty week gestation for a singleton. If you continue to mess with numbers a little more, you can say that "most twins are born early" with many doctors scheduling induction or cesarian sections in the 37-38 week area. This can then cause you to adjust your children's age yet again- they were only two and half weeks early then when compared with most twins, that shouldn't cause any real differences, right???

One might like to think that. One might also like to think that something as minor as a week or two could be made up quickly and without a second thought. I, however, would like to say that you should not plan on this, and you should prepare yourself for a long road of explanations - to yourself, to your extended family, and to strangers on the street. Many medical professionals and baby care books will say that most infants have "caught up" to their developmental age by 24 months. This is to say that you will likely spend the better part of a year or two keeping in check your expectations about when your children should crawl, walk, and talk. Your children may not be "behind" in all areas, you may not notice that they are "behind" at all until later when you're wondering why they are not talking at 12 months like your friend's baby. The truth is, though, that I found the issue of adjusted age specifically identified in a book about assessing readiness for Kindergarten. Even five years later, this author maintained that each week early that a baby was born correlated with one month in delayed maturation, still, at the age of kindergarten entrance. This would mean that a child born 6 weeks early, might be developmentally a half-year "behind" their chronological age when it comes to readiness for school. This might not matter if your child's birthday falls in the first half of the enrollment-age year, but it certainly can if your child is already "young" for the grade.

Adjusted age may haunt you for many years as you watch your children grow and it is best to both keep that in mind and keep it in check. Because nothing is straightforward with child development and the range of "normal" can be quite large, you may not notice a difference between or among your children and others. While keeping age-adjusted expectations in mind might be challenging, but possible, for you and your spouse, you will likely have to remind others- grandparents, friends, and the woman in the grocery store about what is realistic. The truth is that "how old" your babies are will likely be a very common question, followed up by "oh are they doing this or that." You will save yourself a little bit of explanation, depending on who is asking and how much of a difference developmentally you see, by answering with the babies' adjusted age when they're very young. Or, if it's someone you think cares or will understand your explanation, the babies chronological age followed immediately by their adjusted age. Adjusted age and developmental milestones are, of course, most significant when comparing your children to others and to books.

Comparing Children

All parents are likely susceptible to comparing their children to those of their friends, neighbors, and relatives. Parents of multiples, however, have the challenging task of keeping those comparisons in check, while at the same time avoiding comparing their own children. From that first set of statistics- who was born first, how much they weighed and how long they are, you and everyone you know discuss the differences between the children. This is fine, and, perhaps a necessary task even from an evolutionary standpoint. You must "know" your children in any way you can. In the beginning, when your attentions are divided and you sometimes are not sure which baby is crying and cannot remember which baby ate last- perhaps the focus on differences helps you begin to sort out who is who and what is what.

From the lens of the "head game," though, you will want to try very quickly to model behavior that does not compare your children. In our house we chose not to focus on which child was supposedly "born first." We actually did not tell people. I mean, our family knew in the beginning, but we always tried to not make a big deal out of it, and just chose not to share the information with most people. When asked who was older, we would simply say that we never saw it that way or we called it a "tie." We did get a bit of questioning about it, and many people did not understand our rationale. I must admit that this was something I felt strongly about from the time I knew I was pregnant with twins. It was something that never made sense to me growing up- calling a twin older or younger based on a few minutes of difference, or based on who happened to end up positioned below the other, or whose limb was touched first during a c-section birth. Knowing what I did about birth order stereotypes from psychology, I really did not want those stereotypes immediately associated with one of my babies because of what I saw as a random moment in the life of a twin. For us, this little experiment of ignoring standard birth order questions has been a huge success. To be honest, I have to think about it when I want to remember. For us, it just is not a detail that defines our children- to me or to the rest of the world. Now that my twins are old enough to know and answer the "who's older" question themselves, our family's position has remained the same. The kids know, but they also call it a tie. They know that their birth order does not define them.

The only way to win at "The Head Game" is by staying positive. Staying positive is easier written than said, and easier said than done. Life with infant twins can challenge the spirit of even the most optimistic of parents and fatigue, a necessary part of that life, can drain the last drops of positive energy. Staying hopeful- that your babies will sleep for a half hour while you shower, or will gain an all important ounce before their next weight check, or will tolerate their immunizations better than the last round, or will recover from their cold without it getting worse- takes practice, and is most certainly easier on some days than others.

When my babies were little I had a silly little game that I played that helped me get through the week. It's not that I started out making it a game, I just noticed that I was doing it, and then it "became a game." Because I was so tired and didn't get out of the house very much I purchased refrigerator, name-brand, coffee drinks to store at home. Because we were on a budget, they were a treat! Every Monday I would put one in the refrigerator to get cold and each day I would think to myself was today bad enough to warrant a treat or can I make it till tomorrow. If, by Friday, I hadn't yet tapped into my "back-up energy" I would enjoy the drink thinking about how successful I had been that week! Sometimes it really is the small things that get you through the day!

15 JOURNAL: FEB 14TH

Tuesday, February 14th:

Happy Valentine's Day! It seems as though there are fun little things I could write and add to the website everyday. And, actually, I often do compose them in my head while I'm doing multiple other things...the idea being that once I know what I'm going to say, I can just sit down quick and write it! Well, I get all the way to that last part. The "sitting down quick" thing just doesn't seem to happen until I'm laying down in bed at night. And by that time, my mind is off in dreamland.

There's so much I could say about how the babies are doing, that I'm sure I will forget 90% of it now that I'm actually sitting down. The babies turned 5 months old 3 days ago (and they'll be reaching 4 months adjusted age 5 days from now)! We can't believe it. I've probably said this before, but it really is going so fast and slow all at the same time. When we look back, though, at how far we've come it's truly amazing! I mean, I used to spend pretty much all day sitting with them on our "magic pillow" on the couch just to keep them from crying. They used to eat pretty much all the time and we'd be happy to change just a diaper (rather than the whole outfit too)! And now...

Owen is babbling up a storm. He loves to say "ah goo" and make all kinds of raspy sounds in the back of his throat. He speaks to all of his toys (particularly his mobile and the star on his floor gym) in this language and is just pleased as punch when they talk back. Luckily Mike and I do not yet need to have ventriloquism skills to pull off this feat. His latest trick has earned him the nickname "spider monkey" since he's figured out how to push off with his legs while on his back. Putting him on the changing table to change him has become a huge game as he sees how fast he can start moving and whether he can knock anything off the dresser before you can hold it. Because of this, the morning "everyone get changed and dressed" session has moved to the floor where the dynamic duo can move to their hearts' content. Owen has become quite proficient at moving across the floor when he has an objective now (which, interestingly is generally only in his room, so that he can get a better look at his favorite light or so that he can rock the glider, which he just found the other day).

Charlotte has her own set of skills...she prefers to move body parts rather than trying to get anywhere. She will throw her arms and legs all over the place to show her excitement. She does, though, have a patented move whereby she lifts both her legs straight up in the air "Pilates style" (in order to make mom insanely jealous of her abdominal muscles) and then rolls onto her side. She can continue this movement while pivoting around her head which gives her a nice ability to get her feet onto anything within reach (namely, Owen!). Yesterday they were laying parallel on the floor with about a foot in between them. I left them for a second to answer the phone and when I turned back around, Owen had moved himself forward and Charlotte had turned around so that she was kicking Owen in the head. Charlotte is less into the talking thing, preferring that we read her mind. If she feels that we aren't taking her seriously or are taking to long, we'll get some "ah, ah, ah's..."

Overall we're having lots of fun now. We managed to survive our first family illness- didn't help that it lasted a good 2+ weeks. Mom, of course, took the brunt of it as she was the one who continued to not sleep and take care of everyone else! Speaking of sleeping... there have been some dramatic changes recently. We got to a point where the lack of sleeping around here was hitting critical levels. We hadn't managed to achieve any good schedule in the first place, then, pair this with the fact that the babies were getting older and more interested in doing things with us...and we had a recipe for disaster. I think I've described some of their combination killer sleep (or lack there-of) moves in the past. Needless to say, we couldn't get them to bed at night, to nap during the day, if we did get them down, once they woke to eat, they'd be ready to play again... and, mom was tired, and dad was tired of mom being tired, and probably the thing that pushed us the most was that Charlotte and Owen were tired, and we could tell. And, we were spending all day and all night trying to get them to sleep with no success!

So, after consulting with everyone we know as well as the local "Parents of Twins" list-serve, we got the book that everyone on the list-serve recommended, "Healthy Sleep Habits, Happy Child" by Marc Weissbluth. We read it, and are working on implementing and staying consistent with a system. It's not rocket science, true, but, for any of you out there who know how difficult it is to get one baby to sleep, try two. It's tough, too, cause unfortunately there's sometimes more crying involved than I'd like. (Of course, the amount I'd like is zero, so I have to remind myself, that it's protest crying, they're not hurt or in pain). As you can see, sometimes this takes a bit of self-talk to get me through. I have to admit, though, we are seeing dramatic results. We're less than 2 weeks from the initiation of the "plan" and my babies are currently taking nap #2 for the day after sleeping from 6:30/7pm last night to 7am this morning (granted, there were several snacks involved during this timeframe) Now, I should also say that just because they're twins does not mean their personalities are the same- and sleeping styles follow suit. (We'd have a better chance of this if they were identical, though even that isn't a guarantee.) So, there's generally a baby awake all the time still, but, they are at least getting the rest they need whether mom does or not.

Well, I've written a bundle here and I need to accomplish a few more things before napper #1 awakes. Hope you all enjoyed the ramblings as "ah goos," sleep schedules, and radius of kicking has become all consuming to me. We will be happy when winter comes to an end and we can get outside... Ah, going anywhere with twins...that will be the subject of my next installment.

Till next time, and in honor of the Olympics...
Ciao

16 SLEEP

Few subjects receive more attention in the world of new parents than sleep. It is the stuff that humorous commercials, children's books for adults, "forwardable" emails, and desperate posts to parenting message boards are made of. Television shows and movies entertain us with what feels like only slightly exaggerated spoofs of the harried new mother clothed in yesterday's pajamas and hair looking worse only than the exhausted expression across her face. Yes, everyone knows that babies sleep on their own schedule; they don't have their days and nights straight, they miss you, and they have to get on a schedule. Whatever the explanation, the universal truth is obvious- babies do not sleep on the same schedule that the rest of the world does!

Most expectant parents are prepared for this truth, but what this means when you have twins is something entirely different. It doesn't seem to matter whether or not you have had kids before or how good or bad of sleepers you and your husband are. You see, with twins it is truly possible that you will *never* sleep. Accepting this truth from the beginning and understanding that there might be no single larger issue to deal with as a new parent of twins is paramount to your success during your babies first year of life.

There are countless books available solely on the subject of sleep. I recommend that you read any number or all of them. The more you know about sleep before your babies arrive, the more prepared you will be to handle any eventuality. I did not realize that this would have been a wise thing to study up on while I was pregnant, and after four months of very little sleep, I somehow found time to read an entire book (at least twice) on the subject! I asked for recommendations from my local Parents of Multiples group. One title was clearly well liked and I read, re-read, and referenced that book perhaps every half-day during some of the stormiest periods of my children's sleep unrest. I still credit this book with being the foundation on which we've built our family's sleep system throughout my children's development.

Some sleep systems may feel like a better or worse fit for a parent's temperament. Some systems that "feel" better may not actually be better depending on the scenario that presents itself at home. I am convinced, however, about two things. First, choose a system and try to make it work whether or not it is what your friend, neighbor, or mother recommends. And second, if you're not sure whether something is working or you find yourself unable to implement the system that you originally thought felt best, don't be afraid to try something new.

What Makes Sleep So Challenging With Twins

There are a number of reasons that sleep is more elusive with twins. Identifying these reasons will help you understand the challenges that lay before you and should inform your expectations. Understanding the challenges can help you identify solutions to your babies' particular set of circumstances. Sometimes, I'm afraid to say, the solution may just be patience. Sometimes the answer is as simple as waiting for the calendar pages to turn. Learning to identify and frame the challenges in a way that empowers you as a parent to feel in control can go a long way towards giving you the confidence to both survive and take a little more lightly each stage of development.

First, many, if not most twins are born prematurely. Even if you were fortunate enough to carry your twins to term, it is generally accepted that term for multiples is around 37-38 weeks while most singletons are born at 40 weeks. Therefore, at the very least, we're presuming the majority of twins are born 2-3 weeks early. I did not realize until after my babies were already here- and mine made their appearance five and a half weeks early- that even that 2-3 week difference for twins born at "term" was still a very big deal in terms of when they would reach particular developmental milestones. Sleep, it turns out, is one of those easily affected measures. I started joking early on that I was already *"8"* weeks tired but my babies were only *"2"* weeks old. The fact is that humans require sleep and babies who are at worst supposed to still be in utero, or who are at best still functioning in what some authors term the 4th trimester, are used to sleeping on their own schedule. Mixing these two worlds can lead to some very tired parents and, not usually considered, overtired babies. A baby's developmental age has a profound impact on their ability to organize sleep.

Second, it seems obvious enough, but it must be said- you have two babies. It might feel awkward to admit that you think about your babies as a unit, but the truth, at least for me- and especially in the early days when there was so much to be attended to- is that major baby care tasks like feeding and sleeping are generally done with both babies at the same time. You want, no, you need your babies to sleep at the same time, at least most of the time, so that you can also get some rest. For most parents, though, this is a challenge from the beginning. Your babies are, perhaps, biologically inclined towards different sleep patterns. Remember, fraternal twins are only as alike as any other two siblings, they were just born at the same time. Identical twins may be biologically inclined towards the same schedule, but environmental differences- due to growth and size differences in utero, during the birth process, and in the medical care they required after birth- may have altered their rhythms from each other. Though a parent of twins, you must assume that you have two babies with their own unique needs and schedules. While there are steps you can take to move both yourself and your babies towards a happy medium, remembering that there are at least three sets of needs can, perhaps, help you better tolerate the chaos that will surely reign from time to time.

Sleeping at Home

When my babies came home from the hospital they were two weeks old, which left them three and a half weeks shy of their 40-week due date. After I was discharged from the hospital and before the babies came home, I had a set schedule every day to visit them- to maximize the number of feedings I would be present for. Not once during these two weeks did I ever think about how much or how little they were sleeping. The only time I considered sleep at all, in fact, was as we were walking out of the NICU door with the babies in their car seats ready to head home for the very first time. I believe it was a nurse, who literally called after us as our backs were already turned, "Remember they need to sleep on their backs," she said. Now, in the NICU our babies were hooked up to all kinds of monitors, and, as such, they were allowed to sleep on their bellies, snuggled in to lambskin blankets. Just the kind of environment a baby, new to the world, would find comfort in.

Then, however, you take them home. Out of the world they knew and were used to- whether that's right after birth and they are still adjusting to the world outside the womb, or whether they are making a second transition- from womb, to hospital, to home. These worlds are all very different from each other. More so than I ever realized would matter to my babies. The noise level, the lights, the rhythm of the day- these are all very different from one environment to the next. For babies, making these transitions in a matter of days to weeks is very challenging. It will affect both their ability to settle and their ability to remain asleep during lighting and noise-level changes at home.

Where Should They Sleep

Where your babies sleep at home is truly a matter of personal preference, space, and, may I suggest, ease for parents. Whether you have a multi-story home, or a small apartment there are really only a few considerations. First, do you believe they sleep better or worse when together or separate? I have run into a surprising number of strong opinions about this particular matter in my time as a mother of multiples. My personal belief, as is fairly consistent across baby-raising topics, is that there is no "right" or "wrong" way of handling this. I believe it is fairly impossible to separate out why sleep, in this case, is better or worse on any given occasion. Therefore, when thinking about this topic I recommend both trial and error as well as deciding based on what works for the household.

My babies were co-bedded in the NICU, something we pushed for when they were medically ready. It was, perhaps, an emotional decision at first: How could they not miss the person they had spent 34 weeks with? And, how could we leave them alone in an isolette? Indeed, when they were co-bedded, it turned out that their temperature regulation improved, my son seemed to remember to breathe, and, as an added benefit, they were ever so cute!

The second part of the "where should they sleep question" relates to where their bodies actually lay. While I can guarantee you that any newborn will happily sleep in your arms, this particular plan is cute only for so long! At some point your arms will get tired, you will get tired, or you will want to do something important like eat or use the bathroom. Understanding, then, that your "first choice" location is already your babies "second choice" should help you understand why none of this is ever as smooth as it seems like it should be. Some families prefer to sleep near their infants for a while- how long is truly a matter of personal preference and, perhaps, baby and parent temperament. Others prefer that their babies sleep in their crib(s) in their room(s) from the beginning and make use of various monitors- sound, video, etc- to assure them that all is well.

When our babies came home we tried everything. Our original plan was for the babies to sleep together in a single pack-n-play right next to our bed. It was a nice thought, it really was. We'd all go to sleep together and I'd be right next to them if they needed anything. At least that was the plan when we all laid down at bedtime the very first night they were home. I don't actually remember if or how much I slept that night, but I am quite sure that it was not very much. I actually have clear memories of a 3am (or so) flip-out when both babies, myself, my husband, and my mother-in-law who was visiting to help us out were all awake and standing together in the three foot by three foot area that was our hallway. I think the words that came out of my mouth were something to the effect of "someone in this house needs to get some sleep tonight!"

Shortly thereafter we gave up on the idea of sleeping in the bedroom and the babies and pack-n-play moved into the living room with me. As my husband had to work and function each day we decided that it was most important to make sure he was able to sleep without disruption. I started sleeping on an Aerobed which we blew up each night and took down in the morning. Actually, the bed became a running joke, as a kind of metaphor for the type of night and day we were having. We joked that it was a "good day" if the bed was down when my husband came home at night. If the bed was instead still fully inflated, filling up the entire living room, then it was a sign that no one had enough sleep and we spent the entire day trying to get some more!

While the babies started in the pack-n-play together, we quickly decided that they were growing and moving and disturbing each other. To maximize our own sleep we decided to separate them and one remained the pack-n-play and the other moved to a basinet. All three of us remained together in the living room. I wish I could say that this arrangement worked and that we all managed to sleep in between feedings. I'm honestly not sure whether someone just always needed to eat or whether they never wanted to be put down after eating but I was not able to get enough sleep during those early weeks. Actually, "enough" might be the wrong word. I was getting very little at all and my sleep deprivation grew exponentially.

Surviving the Time When There Is No Plan for Sleep

As I'm convinced is true with every stage of child-rearing, there are both positives and negatives to this time when you cannot plan for your babies sleep. First, in those early days and weeks when your babies are asleep, they're quite asleep. This is the time to vacuum their room- sure, right next to their cribs, and cut their fingernails. They won't wake up, they don't really know any better! Second, and perhaps most important for the parents psyche is that no one expects them to sleep at any given time. Most parents avoid making plans when they have a newborn at home. They don't know what their days and nights are going to be like and they plan accordingly. How long parents remain in this stage, however, depends on a number of factors including variables such as whether they need to go back to work on a designated date, whether they have others around to help hold babies while they catch up on their own sleep during the day, and whether they have other children at home that need care during this period of exhaustion.

The downside of these early weeks, more or less depending on both how early your babies are born and on the temperaments of your babies themselves, is obvious. Complete and utter exhaustion is inevitable. The truth is that it is very likely that a baby will be awake almost the entire night. You may get short hour-long bursts of sleep here and there, but we all know that that is not enough on an ongoing basis. It is this early physical stress that I believe snap even the most prepared parents into survival mode. As I have told many a new parent of twins, the most important thing you can do for your own sanity during this hardest time is to lower your expectations- about everything. You cannot expect yourself to have showered, cleaned the house, or even cooked dinner when you are getting so little sleep. It is important for you to try to catch as many naps as you can and sleep in whatever way works best for you so that you can physically manage the essential tasks of parenting. What is truly essential? I would argue that making sure everyone is fed and that babies have periodic diaper changes are the only two things that need to happen in the first weeks of baby care. If you're breastfeeding or pumping you must ensure that you are eating the right kinds and quantities of food and drink to produce enough milk. If those things are being accomplished, then you are doing just fine and should not worry if you remain in your pajamas all day!

That being said, exhaustion is problematic. It can make you feel sick, it can slow down your healing from childbirth and your production of breast milk. It can complicate postpartum hormonal changes that are already in full swing. Most mothers of multiples that I've spoken with have had to come up with a plan to specifically address sleep issues. What you come up with will likely be related to the resources you have- both personal resources- like who is around to help willingly, and financial- how much you can pay to hire help to be around.

At the time we had our babies we had little of either of those resources. So, what I am here to say is that it can be done, it is survivable, and, when accomplished, you will feel all the stronger and more capable for doing it. That being said, if you are on your own, let me be perfectly clear from the get-go that you will get absolutely nothing else done in a day other than get you and the babies food and sleep!

What ended up working for us in the early months was co-sleeping. To be very clear at the outset, co-sleeping is not recommended because of the risk of accidental suffocation. The American Academy of Pediatrics does not recommend bed-sharing. This was not the only "sleep rule" that I broke over the time that my babies were young. But what I believed at the time, and still maintain, is that what we were doing prior to co-sleeping was unsustainable and that was not good for or safe for any of us either. In my mind, I had taken as many precautions as possible to make this a safe sleeping experience for all three of us. Every parent has to evaluate their options and think creatively when it comes to finding time and strategies for sleep.

The babies and I ended up sleeping together on the Aerobed in the living room. It ended up being a "retroactive master plan"- a phrase I borrowed many years ago from a movie I can't recall- defined as a plan where "you don't know what you've done till you've done it and then you realize what a genius you are!" The Aerobed had grooves, like most air mattresses do, and I would first line pillows up and down the sides of the bed, then I would lay each baby in their own groove on opposite sides of the bed. I would lay in the middle. I would then spend the night rolling from one side to the other, nursing whichever baby was hungry and crying. I slept as much as I could (and I was so tired by this point in their lives that I felt like I was mostly asleep most of the time) while they were nursing. The amount of sleep I was getting definitely improved with this system. I will say, though, that at times it feels as though you are never entirely asleep, as I was quite aware of the babies being next to me and the importance of keeping them safe.

When Can I Make a Sleep Plan

By the time my babies were 4 months old, the sleep plan that had worked for us for a few months had become "old." I wanted to go back to my bed and I wanted to pretend, at least, that I was getting more and better sleep. It was at this time that I first realized I did not know nearly enough about babies and sleep and set out to find "the answer." I have said upwards of a hundred times to what feels like as many mothers of multiples that for me, months 4-6 was the very hardest time in terms of getting my babies enough sleep.

Sleep problems abound during these months- both for nap time and for overnights. The babies do not want to nap as much as they used to; they enjoy your company and are beginning to be interested in the world. When they do fall asleep it is not necessarily at the same time as their brother or sister, so it is possible for someone to be up all the time. I remember a time when I wondered if my children specifically planned to sleep opposite each other so that they would both get individual time with me. While that sounds wonderful- to have time to focus on just one child- the truth is that you then lose any time to take care of yourself. At night the problems are even more complicated. Perhaps your babies fall asleep nursing (as mine always did) and then you try to carefully, and generally unsuccessfully, put them into their cribs without them waking up. You can easily become accustomed to spending several hours trying to put your baby to bed for the first time. But, sure enough, they're still waking up overnight to eat, and you then find yourself in the same predicament in the middle of the night.

As a parent, you are so so very tired after four months of constant care. But the truth is that many babies, especially premies, are not entirely ready to organize their sleep just yet. It was during this time, however, that we began to create an order to our daytime sleep. Following the advice of Dr. Weissbluth, we focused on daytime naps and putting the babies down for a nap "within 1-2 hours of wakefulness." Because my babies were frequently up around 6:30am, this meant that their first morning nap would be at 8 or 8:30am. This was definitely counter-intuitive to me, as I assumed that "they had just woken up, they can't be tired just yet!" But, sure enough, the first nap of the day became the most consistent. Both kids ate and fell asleep for at least (or about) 45 minutes. This was the time that I took a shower and ate a meal. Whatever I most wanted to get done I did as soon as the babies fell asleep for their first nap!

I spent those months, it seemed, putting my children to bed, feeding them, and then putting them to bed again! The truth is that when you follow the sleep plan exactly (and I found that my life went much more smoothly when I did) there is not a lot of time left to "do other things." I tried to get out of the house once a week during the weekdays- that was my goal. It was small, yes, but it felt manageable.

What Type of Overall Plan Will Work For Me

The type of sleep plan that will work for you truly depends on a number of factors. If the babies are in the same room, as mine were, then I happen to believe that your choices are more limited. When it comes to night time sleep and teaching the babies to fall asleep on their own, we let them (as used colloquially) "cry it out." Because we waited until the kids were closer to seven months (using their "adjusted age" as a marker for readiness for sleep training) we were very, very exhausted and, as such, wanted a system that would both work and work quickly. We believed what Dr. Weissbluth had written about it being our responsibility to get our children enough sleep and used his method to make it happen. We put the babies to bed, assured ourselves that they were fed, diapered, and otherwise perfectly safe and ready for sleep. We then closed the door to their room and waited for them to fall asleep. Now, this method isn't without disastrous pitfalls-especially for a nursing mother. The very first night I had to leave our apartment and walked down the street to hang out at the grocery store for a while because it was so hard to hear them cry. My son cried for four hours that night the first time we put him to bed. On day two, my son cried for two hours. While still a difficult two hours, even I could see that he went to sleep twice as fast as the day before. On day three, he only cried for thirty minutes. On day four, we put him in his bed and he went to sleep without crying. What I tell every parent struggling with this issue now is this: "If I told you that in four days you would put your babies to bed and they would go to sleep without crying, would you do it?" That experience of "teaching my babies to sleep" has informed me throughout the rest of my parenting. Things that are hard are sometimes still right.

Final Words of Wisdom Regarding Sleep

Do not worry about the babies waking each other up. If you want them to sleep in the same room, keep them together and know that they will get used to each other. In fact, when my babies were little one of them could easily be screaming while the other was sleeping peacefully. It is only later, when they're older, that the other sometimes wakes up to "help" their twin scream too. You know, in case you can't hear the first baby.

Don't be afraid to hear them cry. Sometimes they just need time to settle, sometimes they're just mad. Dr. Weissbluth's book is actually quite good at making you feel guilty for not helping them learn good sleep hygiene. If you start feeling badly, read it again!

If sleep goes better or worse on any given day try not to worry too much about what you did wrong. I have vivid memories of pouring over my "sleep Bible" trying to figure out what it was that I did right or wrong that the kids slept (or didn't) on any given day or time. Sometimes things work and other times they don't. Maybe a baby is starting to teethe. Maybe they're getting sick or maybe they just needed a diaper change at an inopportune time. There just isn't always an explanation.

I always put my kids to bed at the same time. My kids were notoriously bad nappers for their first 18 months and it would at least guarantee me 45 minutes to an hour of kid free time (though I might hear them screaming in the background). I found that if I didn't have that short break without babies I would go crazy (that, and I would have never had a chance to eat or shower).

Be fairly rigid about the nap schedule. Once you find something that works, do everything you can to protect it. Trust me, it is really not worth it to mess up the nap schedule for most things. And, most parents of twins I've talked to are in agreement about this!

If a "schedule" is not working, try something new, but give it a fair try. My kids take a week, sometimes 2 to settle back into a routine when things get shaken up. This is especially difficult to manage because usually I'm so tired from the sleep being messed up that I can't stand giving anything two weeks to work... but it generally does eventually fix itself!

Don't try any new sleep thing while the kids are sick or making any other big changes (like you going back to work).

I always fed my babies at the same time to preserve my sleep. Whenever one got up overnight to eat, I woke the other. My daughter was better about sleeping longer than my son, so every now and then I'd let her sleep and see if she could make it till the next time my son got up. If she did, I'd keep letting her go till she woke up "between feedings." If she woke up in between, I'd start waking her up again. I don't think it mattered to her, because both babies pretty much ate in their sleep anyways!

Don't be afraid to put your kids to bed early. As Weissbluth has drilled into my head: "Sleep begets sleep." The more sleep you get your babies, the better they will sleep.

If you can "sleep when the babies sleep," that's great. If you can't, that's okay too. Sometimes taking a shower or eating some lunch will make you feel even better.

17 JOURNAL: MAR 5TH

Sunday, March 5th

The babies will be 6 months old on Saturday and Mike and I can't stop commenting on the fact that we can't believe it's been half a year already that they've been here with us. Boy a lot has changed and I find myself thinking about how far we've come and how much further I'd like to be all at the same time. Essentially, I've become a walking cliché.

The babies are so much fun to be around at this point. When they're awake, they are generally happy and playful. They've both figured out how to scoot around on their backs wherever they're put down. They still prefer to do this with as little clothing as possible for the best traction. We think they're going to enjoy the warmer weather immensely. They've both demonstrated that they can roll from front to back and back to front at this point. Charlotte is pretty obsessed with the back to front roll and will flip over quite frequently (a favorite time being in the middle of a diaper change). In her excitement over mastering this feat, she seems to have temporarily forgotten how to roll back the other direction (which she accomplished first). So, when she grows tired of being on her stomach, she begins to complain.

Owen prefers moving to rolling. He will, however, roll half-way over while playing and just last night I saw him experiment with that in his crib. I will be happy when he can roll back and forth easily so that he is more comfortable at night!

We're not sure how much the babies weigh at this point, but they're getting big. We've spent the whole weekend (it seems) trying to figure out how to adjust and install their new carseats, as they've grown out of the infant ones. This means, of course, that they've now graduated to riding in the stroller facing front in the regular seats, rather than in the snap-in carseats. We went for our first walk yesterday with them in the regular stroller seats. We think they were pretty much freaked out the whole time…but, they didn't cry, so maybe it was growing on them!

Everyone keeps asking us if they've started solid food yet… they've got a little bit longer to wait, cause we're waiting till 6 months from their due date to introduce food. We're hoping to stack the odds in our favor to prevent food allergies, especially since Owen has already showed a sensitivity to dairy products. So, April 19th is the target date. I'm sure it will be here in a flash.

The sleeping thing is going better overall, though teething and Owen's love of food continues to sabotage my attempts at a full night's sleep. (A full night, who am I kidding, 4-6 hours uninterrupted would be great!) I've pretty much memorized the book we got to help us problem solve every little change in their sleeping patterns. And, overall, I think we know what we're doing and just need to let them grow and develop a little more.

Mom and dad are hanging in there. The babies are loving having Mike at home more on the weekends, which we both think explains their lack of desire to nap on Saturdays. His schedule has finally moved towards regularity and he's done all his hard months. Two more overnights this month, and he'll be completely done with that till the end of residency. What will happen at the end of June? Not sure yet, but we'll let you know when we do.

As a final note, we love to have visitors so if you ever want to come say "hi," please call or email us! We haven't really got our acts together to initiate invitations, but we're more than happy to entertain! The current nap "schedule" also makes it tough for us to get out of the house for long, so we're a big fan of having people here rather than going out.

Happy End of Winter, Everyone!

18 TAKING CARE OF YOURSELF

With two babies to care for it might seem counter-intuitive to have a chapter dedicated to taking care of yourself. But, as difficult as it is, taking care of mom is essential to being able to care for your babies.

PHYSICAL WELL-BEING

The early days post-delivery were generally a fog for me. I delivered via c-section and left the hospital with pain, post-surgery instructions, and a husband who had to drive and help shuttle me everywhere. The recovery was more difficult than I anticipated, further complicated by my back and forth to the hospital every day. As my abdomen recovered I paid more attention to the pain from nursing- the pumping was taking a toll on my breasts and a host of creams and gel packs were the only thing keeping me going. Those hurdles were crossed early, though, and my expectations were that I would lose weight rapidly, move back into regular clothes, and generally feel myself again in short order.

It turns out that the physical recovery was complicated by a lack of sleep, an inability to shower, let alone exercise, and an overwhelming desire to stress-eat. I had my days of "getting it together," where I would shower during the kids first nap (to make sure I got one, no matter what happened with nap) and then would attempt to do my Pilates video. These attempts to "get my body back" were both sporadic and slightly futile. I was in the midst of an experience unlike no other I had been through before, one which did not lend itself to reclaiming my body.

When the babies were about six months old I realized that I needed that find some pants that were not maternity wear (though I must admit to being a huge fan of comfortable maternity pants). I did not want to spend money on clothes that I did not expect to be in long-term, still believing that I was in a temporary state which would soon return to normal. I had friends tell me (about their singleton pregnancies) 9 months on, 9 months off, but somehow that seemed longer than it could possibly take!

Well, it turns out that it can take at least that long- and how long really depends on what measures you count. Some things to think about and watch for over your recovery:

Eating Enough:

While you may have a desire to lose every baby pound quickly and you may wonder how anyone has time to eat while caring for newborn twins, it is very, very important to be deliberate about your food choices. If you are nursing twins you must make sure that you ingest enough good, nutritional, calories so that you can produce good breast milk. You should also specifically make sure you are getting enough good fats. Along with that, you must continue to drink a large amount of water, all day long. You want to establish and maintain a good milk supply. You want your milk to be there when your babies are hungry and want enough to fill them up and help them gain weight. Nursing will gradually help you lose weight, but this is not the time for you to try to do so.

Separated Abdominals:

Carrying twins puts a huge amount of stress on your body and abdomen. Sometimes you can develop a condition called *diastasis recti* where after birth your abdominal muscles, which separated to make room for the babies, do not migrate back to the middle. No amount of sit-ups and crunches will slim down your middle if you have this condition. While generally regarded as a cosmetic issue, for parents of twins who are lifting lots of pounds of baby, left untreated this condition can lead to back problems- especially as your babies get bigger and heavier.

A way of testing to see if you have abdominal separation can be done at home. Lay on your back with your knees bent and feet flat on the floor. Place your fingers over your stomach, just below your belly button. Lift your head and neck off of the floor, raised only slightly. If multiple fingers can fit into the opening you may have diastasis. If you believe you have this condition, speak to your physician for more information. A referral for physical therapy can be very helpful in correcting this condition. I was referred to physical therapy when my babies were about 18 months old for back pain I could no longer tolerate. After figuring out that core instability (as a result of my separated abdominal muscles) was the cause of my back pain, I saw dramatic results in just eight weeks doing one very simple exercise. I wished I had taken a picture of my stomach before and after physical therapy- the change in shape was really dramatic.

Body Changes:

There is not much that doesn't change when you are pregnant with twins- your face, your belly, your backside, your hips- weight gets put on, it comes off, and it's never really where it was before- at least not for a while. While many mothers of twins are too busy to change clothes, let alone look in the mirror, every now and then you might find yourself evaluating your post-twin body and wondering what happened! The truth is that depending on your child care situation, your motivation, the amount of sleep you get, the number of hours in a month you have to yourself, and a whole host of other factors, you may not find the time to put into you that you want. You may find yourself going through several seasons, or several years, wearing a small wardrobe, not wanting to invest in pieces that you don't plan to need by the next season.

In my experience it took years before I had the right cluster of timing, motivation, and will power to add back exercise and healthy eating to my life. In my experience, the days took all of the energy that I had to give and there was nothing left to spend on myself. While this is not, of course, the recommended path to take, it is the one that many women do. And, while sometimes it is okay to have goals take years, it is important not to lose sight of the ultimate goal. Your babies need you to be healthy and need you to take care of yourself. Keep that in mind as they grow older and look for ways to insert exercise into your life with them. Teach them to eat healthy by example and know that all of this will take time to implement.

EMOTIONAL WELL-BEING

Where physical, mental, and emotional well-being and health collide, and where they diverge is not always clear. The convergence of the three, however, influence how new parents behave and feel. This, in turn, defines just how well the parents cope with all of life's changes.

Hormonal Changes:

While hormones are technically a physical issue, the rapid change in various hormonal levels that mothers experience after delivery very much impact their emotional health. Just as you may have experienced a more extreme level of sickness and emotions at the start of your twin pregnancy, so too might you find a rocky path back to your normal levels. Emotional lability is common and completely normal after delivery. After childbirth you will see a dramatic reduction in estrogen and progesterone levels. How your body copes with these changes in hormone levels will dictate the degree your mood may be affected. Allow yourself the flexibility of getting upset and know you won't feel that way forever. Ask your husband, partner, and family to give you some "extra love" and understanding during a time when you might need it. You may find that nursing or pumping is helpful in mitigating some of these negative hormonal issues as it stimulates the release of other hormones.

Facing Reality:

You have spent months, and perhaps years, preparing for the birth of your babies, and you have likely thought about being a parent for many more. All of the expectations- hopes and dreams for your babies and your experience as a parent-have come to life and it is possible that reality does not meet expectation. This can be a difficult adjustment to make if you are not prepared for it. Caring for infant twins is challenging, it takes practice, patience, and sometimes, an iron will. The most important thing to remember is that the hard of the moment won't continue forever. Focusing on meeting your babies basic needs- feeding them repeatedly and helping them get to sleep is your primary role. They do not need more from you right now and by the time they do, you will be ready to give it. When you are so tired you can barely see straight, all you need to do is nurse or feed them quietly while you rest your own eyes.

There is no perfect parent, and never was- of a singleton, let alone of twins! You may not change your babies', or your own, clothes as much as you thought you would, and you might have thought you'd be showering and applying make-up sooner than you are. You may not have expected to have trouble getting to the grocery store, or even to periodic doctor's appointments. You might find that life with infant twins is nothing like you expected. You might find that you don't exactly even like what you are doing each day. You might find that none of your friends or family understand or appreciate what you are doing all day or why it is hard. You might find yourself far more alone than you expected, despite the babies all over your home!

If you find yourself in this place, one in which your reality is not what you expected, take heart. Know that you are part of an army of mothers and parents of multiples who have found themselves in this exact same place. Making peace with where you are at and knowing that you are doing your best is the first step towards enjoying your real life with babies. Lower your expectations, for yourself and for your babies. Figure out what you need to be fulfilled- is it acknowledgement from others that you're working hard? Is it acceptance of yourself that your best is good enough even if it's not the best that you expected to have? Is it reinforcement that you're not alone? Is it help seeing all that you are accomplishing? Know that your experience is unique, but the challenges are shared by many others who have been in, and will be in, your shoes. Finding people you can relate to to fulfill these needs can go a long way towards melding your expectations with reality.

Avoiding Isolation:

Everyone has a different threshold for how much socialization they need to stay upbeat and positive, but social support helps everyone. Infant twins can challenge even natural homebodies to feel alone and isolated. A constant series of infant needs can make it virtually impossible to leave the home in the early months. Despite this, however, there are a lot of ways to stay in contact with others and to find friends and confidants- that you can meet in person or can exchange stories with online. I cannot overstate the importance of sharing your twin-parenting experience with others who are in the trenches with you- it can go a long way towards making you feel like your experience is both normal and "fun." Frequently, with twins, it can take a retelling of a situation or an understanding that others are experiencing the same joys and frustrations to enjoy the moments. Camaraderie with others, but especially with other parents of multiples, can significantly increase your feelings of well-being.

MENTAL HEALTH

Some parents have struggled with mental health issues their entire lives and may be under ongoing care by a doctor or another mental health professional. If this is true for you, you should be especially mindful of how you are doing after the babies are born and talk with your provider about the best way to monitor your moods during this long postpartum period of transition. It is best to have this plan in place prior to the birth of your babies and to share this plan with your partner and any other trusted friends who can also help you and the babies if necessary.

Some parents may find themselves struggling for the first time after their babies are born and may not know what to do or who to talk to. If you are not sure if your moods and emotions are normal responses to what you have been through, or, if you think they are normal but find that they are disrupting your life- your work, your home, your ability to enjoy your new babies- you should seek the advice of a doctor or mental health care provider. Some jumble of emotions is normal following birth, but the duration and intensity of these symptoms vary. It is really important to address any concerns you may have early on so that you can seek treatment to manage your symptoms and enjoy your babies.

19 JOURNAL: MAR 24TH

Friday, March 24th

Charlotte & Owen continue to do well... they continue to put on the pounds and grow through their clothes! Owen is quite good these days at rolling over, though can still surprise himself when he "over-rolls" and ends up on the same side he started on! Charlotte has temporarily forgotten how to roll from front to back and has instead been working on propelling herself into the air in sort of inverse hopping fashion- like a frog, but on her back! They've both got their own adorable vocalizations (most of which resemble dolphin sounds). Owen squeals with delight when he's happy and will carry on a good conversation if he's got some things on his mind. Charlotte will quietly, but seriously, tell you the secrets to the universe if she's in the proper mood after a good meal.

Speaking of meals... we'll be starting to experiment with solid foods real soon, as they've just started showing interest in our food. Charlotte, particularly, is enamored with ice water- the way the ice clinks in the glass... she just has to reach out to grab it (that, and anything else that might be in our hands). I've let her try to drink from my glass- she looks like a little kitten, trying to lap up the water with her tongue. While most of the water ended up on me she had a ball at the attempt and didn't want to stop!

Well, Owen just had his mid-evening snack (the one between dinner at 6:30 and his midnight snack), which means it's time for me to quick get to bed before the night games begin. One last quick story that relates to this, though... I went to the mall today briefly (as all our trips are), but met up with a classmate of Mike's who has 10-month-old twins (the spectacle that we usually are when out in public was magnified x10). We then passed a woman who was there with her 1-year-old twins... her first question to me was, "Are you sleeping yet?" To which, of course, I said "no." Ah, a moment of empathy and connection between strangers.

And with that story (that probably no one found as interesting as me), I'm off to bed!

20 GETTING THROUGH THE DAY

When you're home with baby twins, any given hour can flow into the next without you being real sure what happened to it! Some days can feel long, others short- generally this depends on how well the babies nap and whether those naps occur at the same time! If you wake up feeling ready to conquer the world, the day can go much differently than if you wake up in a haze. Some days you won't care what you do, but other days you will need to actually be somewhere at a certain time or accomplish something specific.

After the first few months you may find that a somewhat regular rhythm appears in your day. You'll have a better sense of when you want to get the babies to nap and when they'll be hungry and want to eat. This structure, loose though it may be, can be helpful when the days seem long and still slightly unwieldy. Some days can be trying and, for me, a phone call to another mother of twins in the morning or during that last hour while I waited for my husband to return home, would offer me some much-needed perspective and pep. Getting out of the house can offer a fresh perspective, particularly when others help remind you how cute your babies are. Some days will feel wonderful, and on others you might not be able to shake the funk you are in. Some days the babies will be cranky (maybe they are sick or teething) and some days they will be all smiles. All of these days are normal and should be expected.

There really is no sure-fire way to make the days go smoothly, but if there is one, overarching way to head, it's towards preparation. Preparation of all sorts can, and should, be done while the babies are sleeping- either during naps or at night before you go to bed. If they are awake, you will be distracted and likely holding one, or both, of them. The following tasks will go much more smoothly and will make your life easier if you generally always have them done, and if you do them while the babies are asleep.

Repack the diaper bags:

I remember when I first got my diaper bags- I was so excited, and yet I had no idea what to put in them! Over time you will come up with a system of what you need, and how much of it, for differing lengths of time away from home and the various activities you will be doing. Some items you can store in your bags, ready whenever you need them. Some items you will likely be moving either from bag to bag or need to grab from the refrigerator (pumped milk, ice pack, water bottle, etc). For the regular things, I knew where each went in my diaper bag, and therefore knew what was missing when a spot was empty. For the items that moved around or needed to be added last minute, I taped a list of them to my door so that I would always look at it on the way out (do I have my wallet? phone? keys? etc). I later saw an idea of printing a list of the items you might need to refill or add frequently and attach it to your diaper bag on a luggage tag. A clever idea, and one that allows the list to travel with you!

Food Preparation:

Again, whatever you do while the babies are asleep will allow you two hands and will make tasks go much faster. Any food preparation that you can do in advance- everything from filling a pot with water and setting it on the stove to boil later, to chopping vegetables for salads that you throw together (one handed) later, to putting together bottles and sippy-cups, to setting out, literally everything to make a meal (spices with measuring spoons, boxes of pasta and jars of sauce) will make your life easier. Further, whether your babies are awake or asleep, always turn on a timer when you turn on the oven or stove. There are just too many distractions around when there are baby twins in the house. You must take precautions to back-up your brain and insure that you remember to turn the oven and stove off after using them!

Always have a back-up plan in case your day goes crazy. That might mean a folder with food delivery options, or it might mean a bag of frozen tortellini in the freezer. Tortellinis can be cooked in 3 minutes once the water is boiling; add a jar of sauce on top (pre-heating the sauce is optional!). Done.

Moving Things Around:

Cleaning the kitchen, washing bottles, sorting/ washing/ folding laundry, and taking anything from one room or part of your home to another is best done while the babies are sleeping. Never underestimate how far they'll slither under your feet, how much they won't want you to put them down, or how needy they will be if you plan to accomplish a necessary task while they are awake. If it doesn't have to be done, no big deal. If it does, plan it early and do it during a nap time the day before.

The best tip for getting through each day? Keep your life as simple as possible. Make basic meals; make extra so that you always have leftovers. Plan your day with lots and lots of extra time between places you need to be so that you always have time for an extra feeding when someone is hungry or full clothing change when a diaper explodes. Keep yourself calm and your expectations in check. Remember that for your babies the day is the experience, it's not the things you are doing.

21 JOURNAL: MAY 2ND

Tuesday, May 2nd

Holy smokes- where to begin! You know, it's not like I wait all that long to update the website… I just do it when I have a moment to take a breath, which happens to be between major events in our lives!

This past month has been a whirlwind of activity. At this point, I'm sure you expect nothing less. After we determined that we'd be settling in here in Michigan, we began the house hunting process. I'll sum up that experience as ridiculous. Between real estate agents, bankers, hundreds of online listings, and coordinating touring properties with Mike's and the babies' schedules….it was quite an experience. But, I am pleased to announce that we are soon to be the proud owners of a gorgeous house. We close on May 30th and are counting down the days.

The babies have been rock stars during the whole house

hunting process and subsequent million of errands, meetings, etc. They've spent quite a bit of time in their Baby Bjorns (which are life savers) smiling away at everyone they see and offering squeals of delight and screams of annoyance when necessary. Needless to say, we are a spectacle. Everyone wants to say hello- from the entire staff at the bank, to the appliance salesmen at Sears, to the shark-like staff at the furniture store. What other 7 month olds can say that they've been this involved in the house buying process?

The babies are great. We feel like their personalities are just blooming. In just the past 2-3 weeks even they've become so much more responsive to their environment, wanting to interact with everyone and everything. They've got little GPS radars on the remote controls and the telephones now, and are happy to take them from you (to eat, of course) when you're done using them. Charlotte is pretty able to sit up by herself for a bit now- she can steady herself as she loses balance, but still frequently ends her sitting sessions with a forward-face-plant. Owen is working on the sitting thing and can keep the bottom half of his body in the right position, with a pretty large lean forward from the top half. Hey, we're working on it! They've been eating solid foods now since, well, I think the beginning of April. They've got a diet of rice cereal, sweet potatoes, butternut squash, carrots, peas, applesauce, and a new feature...banana! We're also working on the cup. They love drinking out of mommy's glass, but that generally requires a wardrobe change for both baby and mama afterwards. Charlotte is able to suck the water out of the sippy cup at times, but both babies seem to think that the spout makes a much better teether than functional cup.

It was a big month for the babies- they got to see all their grandparents! Grandma and Grandpa B. came up to visit us right after we bought the house and we took a "little" trip to Boston to see Grandma and Grandpa M. at the end of the month when Mike had some vacation time in his schedule. Let me tell you, a 14 hour car trip with 7 month olds…we may be certifiably crazy. Actually, it went as well as it could have. On the way there we left at 6pm and pulled in at 8am… totally exhausted. We drove all night and the babies did overall wonderfully sleeping in the car. We were totally shot, though, and decided to make the trip back in 2 days. Still left at 6pm but got a hotel room in order to sleep a few hours before resuming driving. Funny story about that… we got a king size bed so we could just put the babies in bed with us, and wouldn't have to deal with putting up their cribs. Well, Charlotte and Owen thought that was just SO much fun that they woke right up and were ready to play at 1am. Needless to say, it took awhile to get them calmed down and back asleep. We had fun in Boston- the babies, and Mike, got to celebrate their first Patriot's Day. The babies especially enjoyed the parade.

Well, as always, I forget 90% of the things I want to tell everyone in these little letters. But, as my brain is currently fried, I think I'd better think about some sleep, and not try to recover the lost 90%.

22 GETTING OUT & ABOUT

DAY TRIPS

In seventh grade English class I read the book "Cheaper by the Dozen." I can't really remember what the book was about at all, except that the father was an efficiency expert and the family had 12 children because everything was "cheaper by the dozen." I saw the later-released movie that was made with the same title when it came out, and I must admit that there were no sparks of recognition with the storyline. Suffice it to say, that book created an impression on me, and with whatever basis in reality there was- I was forever destined to be an efficiency expert myself! I don't like to backtrack when I'm doing errands, I don't like to go out of my way one day when I'll be in the same area the next, and I certainly like to be on time.

I've had more than enough contact with people who use their children as their excuse for plan changes, lateness, and the like. Not that all of that isn't sometimes appropriate with children, I have just always planned to do my best to minimize this. Having twins, then brought a whole new ridiculousness to planning ahead, getting places on time, and remaining "efficient."

Getting out and around with two infants can try even the most patient of souls. When you are struggling to simply make it through each and every day, though, leaving the house for a doctor's appointment, let alone a cross country trip, can seem like an impassible mountain. Whether trying to accomplish a short errand or make arrangements to get somewhere at a certain time you will find that with practice all is possible.

Make a Plan that Can Work

While it might seem absurd, the obvious must be stated. Juggling the needs of two babies and forcing them onto a schedule that may not be of their choosing is tricky and a workable plan is essential for any chance of success! As with all infant-care tasks, having a firm grip on your expectations is key. You must know what is essential and what is not. Getting to a doctor's appointment for a weight check is essential, picking up diapers is essential (though can be done via online ordering and mail if you plan ahead!), picking up a few things at the grocery store for dinner when there is cereal in the cupboard is not. While a little extreme, my point is obvious.

One of the universal tasks of pregnancy is installing car seats into your car so that you are prepared for that day when you go into labor and will want to take your babies home from the hospital. Preparing for every other trip out of the house with your babies will likely not be quite as easy! I learned the key to leaving the house with twins many years ago in Girl Scouts- Be Prepared! What exactly "being prepared" means when you have twins depends on the situation. The short version, though, is that you should think through each situation, figure out at least a half dozen ways that your plans can get derailed, and plan for those eventualities. I have a note that I wrote when my babies were still babies where I said that I am "living life eight steps ahead of myself." It might seem rather negative to focus on or anticipate the problems of the day. I found, however, that I was much more calm and could enjoy the moments when I felt prepared for whatever the day may bring.

The key to successful travel of any distance with any number of babies is to identify the unchangeable points and the roadblocks to making it to those points. A doctor's appointment at a specific time is unchangeable, roadblocks to making it there can be unhappy, screaming babies who need to be fed, diapered, or held. Traffic can throw you behind, as can a phone call and forgetting several items you need when packing up the car. Planning ahead takes on an entirely different meaning when trying to successfully leave the house with your babies! When your days with infants already feel full and possibly overwhelming, knowing when and how to leave the house is key.

It would be remiss of me to avoid mentioning that no matter how good your plan is, sometimes it just won't work. A baby spikes a fever, both babies are far too upset and tired to be cooperative, or any number of other things can go wrong that there just isn't a fix for. Part of being prepared is knowing that at any moment you may have to abort your mission and try again another day. Maybe you realize this before you even leave the house, it's okay to decide that it's not going to work that day. Maybe you've done all the work to get two infants into the mall- when they both start screaming for food. One of my long told stories is just this- after struggling to get the babies into the car and into the mall on my own, everyone was upset and inconsolable. After trying, and failing, to get the screaming under control we just had to leave and come home. It wasn't pretty, but it was an essential lesson in understanding that not everything can be controlled.

When to Go Out

The essential infant care tasks such as feeding, diapering, and napping, generally get disrupted in some way when going out, so I found it sanity-saving to challenge my children to this flexibility only once a day. Infant needs, multiplied, are always inconvenient with regard to leaving the house and the secret to early success is to plan short trips. For a good while, it is really only realistic to expect to go one place on any given half-day, that is, loading the babies into and out of the car one time. It is only later, perhaps around a year and a half that I could occasionally get to two different locations during one outing. If you have a choice, trips should always be planned for the longest waking period your children have everyday. For the first year, at least, this is generally in the late afternoon- after all the napping is done for the day. A caution here, though, is that this time period can often run into the cranky time of day. Between five and fifteen months, our best window for excursions was generally sometime in the 3pm-5pm window.

As your babies sleep schedules organize you may find other pockets of the day that are convenient to use. Some babies are flexible with where and when they sleep and others are less so. Knowing your babies takes time and their needs will change as they grow. Continuing flexibility on the part of the parents and caregivers are key to adapting and changing with your babies- and key to successful trips out of the house! A final word of caution on timing. Some babies always fall asleep in the car and some babies do not. Some babies continue to sleep just fine in their car seats when they arrive home and some do not. Some babies can be transferred to their cribs after falling asleep in the car and will not wake up, while others will wake up and believe their nap is over! Learning your babies cues, knowing that some days will go smoothly and others will not, and keeping your expectations for adventure on par with where your babies are developmentally at will go a long way towards your feelings of success.

How to Leave the House

Once upon a time, before there were babies, when you wanted to leave the house you picked up your keys, maybe your phone or purse, threw on a jacket, and walked out the door. You had hands available to lock the door behind you and an empty car where you could stash your gear. No part of going anywhere required more than a passing thought. Oh how things change with kids!

No matter the age of your babies, though especially true in the early months, the key to getting out the door and arriving at your destination is to do this directly after they have been fed. This means that all preparatory work like packing the diaper bag, confirming directions to the location and event details, and dressing and primping mom and babies should be done prior to feeding. If you do this, you will have the maximum amount of time available to get somewhere or accomplish something before your babies are hungry again!

My rule of thumb for arriving anywhere on-time was to always plan for three disasters- if you don't use them, you'll be early, if you do, you can still arrive on schedule. A good "back of the hand" average for how many disasters I used per trip? Probably 1.5! These disasters could be anything from a diaper blow-out (or two) to a traffic jam and everything in between. In general I allotted 10 minutes per disaster for a combined "disaster margin" of 30 minutes. This means that if I needed to be somewhere at 4pm I would work backwards to calculate my departure time- 10 minutes to get the kids into and out of the car + 20 minutes to drive there. The "average person" would leave at 3:30pm, but if you're going to live by my 3 disasters rule, you will leave at 3pm. I always prided myself on arriving (with my twins) on time and this rule of thumb kept me right where I wanted to be.

Physically getting your babies ready to leave the house can be more tricky than you might imagine. After making sure your babies are fed and dry, you need to get them strapped into their car seats and loaded into the car. If you are getting your babies ready on your own, these tasks can be challenging to complete quickly (so no one gets too hot or cold) and safely (easier if if your car is inside an attached garage and harder if it is across a parking lot at an apartment complex). What you can do with them initially will also get harder as they get older and gain weight. For the first 9 months of my babies lives we lived in a 3rd floor, walk-up, apartment. We paid extra for a carport so that we had a designated, covered parking spot for the car the babies rode in. This allowed me freedom from scraping snow off my car all winter, and a little bit of benefit when it was raining. It did not make the process of getting the babies into the car any easier. Even when they were little I could never carry both car seats up and down the stairs at the same time. While recovering from my c-section and with the initial weight of the car seats without the babies it became clear that each baby would have to go up the stairs on their own. What an impossibly difficult thing to figure out! If I wanted to do anything by myself it was going to require leaving one baby alone while carrying the other to the car. When I first started experimenting with ways to make this happen I would carry each baby as far as I could while still seeing the other. So, I would carry one baby to the sidewalk while getting the other out of the car. Then I would carry the babies, landing to landing, up the stairs to our apartment. It was not smooth and it was not easy, but it worked. As the babies got older and heavier, and then especially when they switched into convertible car seats which did not lift out of the car, I would leave one in their crib and run the other all the way down and out to the car and strap them in. I would then lock the car and run back up the stairs to get the other from the crib and back down to the car. Again, not ideal, but it was workable. We were fortunate to be able to move when the babies were nine months old- right about the time it was starting to get warm again. I used to tease my husband that we had to find a new place to live because it was getting warm and I wasn't going to be able to leave one baby in the car anymore! I don't find any of these scenarios to be ideal, but they were workable, which is all I had available to me at the time. You must create plans and systems for leaving the house that will work with whatever circumstances you have. Even if you're able to carry two car seats- what about diaper bags, purses, and any other gear you want to have available in the car? You will become practiced at the order of operations you must preform before any trip out of the house.

With the actual "planning" and "leaving" being so hard, why then would anyone want to leave the house? It is easy to imagine that the babies could be well cared for and content within the confines of your living room, let alone the whole apartment or house, and especially in contrast to around town. During the babies first year in general, and first half-year, in particular, the benefits of leaving the house are centered around the parent or caregiver. You can love your babies to the moon and back, but that does not change the sometimes drudgery of full-time infant care. What taking your babies out into the world allows is a chance for you to see those babies the way others see them.

Coping with the seemingly endless array of questions from strangers passing-by can get tiring, but it is also a time for you to take a breath and celebrate your accomplishments. When someone asks "how do you do it?" Know they are asking because they are impressed that you are caring for your babies so competently. When someone says, "they're darling," take a moment to look at each baby, smile, and think so too. When someone watches you competently placing a pacifier in one baby's mouth, while juggling the other into a front carrier, know that you're impressing a handful of people trying not to watch. Yes, sure, there will be days when you drop the pacifier and realize you've forgotten the front carrier (which, incidentally, should always be packed in the stroller basket for just this type of occasion). But, so too will there be days when your babies actually stop crying with, what some on-lookers might describe as a wave of your hand. The "mommy magic" happens, at times, and you should feel proud. Taking your babies out in the world truly highlights all that you can do.

If you stay home with your babies during the day, the hours can feel long and the quiet can grow loud. I often enjoyed the chance to speak to other adults, if only in the check-out line. I enjoyed the chance to let my babies be admired, if only from a distance (as I was rather rigid about germs)! Getting out makes your brain work, it challenges your planning abilities, and it gives your body a chance to move- something it does not do much of when you are home and nursing. Start small, practice, and know that getting out enough means, probably, just once in a while.

Getting Inspired to Go Out Solo

Sometimes the hardest part of leaving the house is getting up the will and motivation to do so. When there are equal numbers of adults and babies, leaving the house might be seen as a manageable adventure. It is when you are home alone that it is perhaps even more important to practice venturing out. Each successful solo trip you take will increase not only your confidence, but your skills and "toolkit" for fixing problems that arise when you are out. I have met parents of twins who are in their toddler and preschool years who have never taken their children out of the house by themselves. I believe that it is very important that you do so from the beginning, so that you feel in control of the situation and can learn to bend and flex as required. Parents who work full time have an even trickier time, as their opportunities for this type of practice are more limited. I would argue that handling both babies solo- both inside the home and out- is a worthwhile priority.

When you are so very tired as it is, and a task seems like more trouble than it is worth, it is easy to feel like the task is just too big to tackle. Starting early on with small trips can help you build confidence and practice the skills you will use forever when it comes to taking your children out of the house. As I have said on any number of occasions throughout this book, keeping your expectations low is the most important part of being successful. When my babies were young we tried to leave the house once a week. It probably seems rather absurd to those who have not lived with newborn twins, but that seemed to me to be the amount I could handle. If most of the week had gone by and I hadn't left the house, I made a point to. When you're balancing a lack of sleep and an effort to get dressed, with the supposed benefits of getting out of the house, the equation is sometimes not as balanced as you might like.

Where to Go

It is helpful to have a good reason to leave the house-someone you're meeting or a fun reward (like a hot coffee or tasty dessert!) at the end of it. The grocery store down the street was a key destination for my double stroller full of babies and myself. I would enjoy a seven-layer bar from bakery while I wandered around the store, picking up whatever rations would fit in the stroller basket and browsing magazines as long as the babies had patience. It was a small trip, manageable for the time in between feedings and not so far that I couldn't make it home if everyone got severely upset at once. In the early months you are leaving the house for yourself- so accomplish something, or not, as you desire. Treat yourself to food that someone else prepared or walk around a store that you enjoy being in. Sometimes getting a little exercise walking the corridors of the mall can be a pick-me-up, and sometimes a stroll through the baby clothes section of the local baby superstore can bring a smile to your face.

As the babies get older, you can tailor your trips out more for them. Libraries often hold baby playgroups, with a short program of songs, stories, and games for the under-two set to enjoy, possibly followed by an open playtime when parents can socialize while their babies explore new toys and surfaces. Museums tailored towards children frequently have an area for infants and toddlers to enjoy and your babies might do well taking in the sights and sounds. My babies often napped very well following excursions, something which reinforced the extra effort of taking them out of the house! During the first year of a babies life you should never worry about "stimulating" them in any particular way. The world is all new and everything is exciting.

OVERNIGHT TRAVEL

At some point in your babies' lives, you will need to go somewhere overnight. Some families do this sooner and some families do this later and it likely depends on where the babies' grandparents live! All of our family was out of state, so we began our overnight travel lives early on and took three major trips before our babies were 12 months old. Our first overnight trip was for the babies' first Christmas- when they were 3.5 months old (or, 2 months, adjusted). It was a 3.5 hour drive that probably took twice that long. We stopped on more than one occasion to nurse on the way there, and we still were not getting any sleep at night (at home or during the trip!). I can't say that I have wonderful memories of that trip. But, we did it. Our second overnight trip was when the babies were 7 months old. It required an 11.5 hour drive, plus stops.

We had the idea that we would drive all night and hope the babies slept for a good portion of that time. They did, but we wanted to also. We never drove overnight again, deciding it was far too dangerous for all of us. As I mentioned earlier, the key to having the motivation to do crazy things like this is to have a good reason at the end of it. In our case, we were visiting both sets of grandparents who were thrilled to have the babies visit their homes! Our third trip was another cross-country car trip when the babies were 10 months old. We were heading to visit our newborn twin nephews and all of our extended family. By that time we were packing baby food, still nursing, and our babies had just started sleeping consistently through the night. Nothing like messing up a new routine!

Having What You Need

It can be challenging to anticipate what you need for an afternoon, let alone an overnight or more. Being prepared with all of the supplies and baby gear you need for a trip will make your life much easier and how you transport or obtain what you need is a matter of time, space, and resources. The truth is that I have always felt like whether you were leaving for just one day, or for however many after that, the amount of stuff you needed did not change significantly. Once you pack, you're ready for anything. The most important tool for packing is to have a good list that you can update by the event and as your babies grow. I recommend that you update this list electronically and then print it out approximately one week prior to the trip. You will continue to think of new things to add to the list over that week- as you live your life and care for your babies. It will be most handy to have the list available for reference and note-taking. This list will go with you on your journey and serve as your reminder for collecting all of the gear you brought with you before returning home! If you found you needed something you didn't have, add it to the list as well. Upon returning home, I suggest electronically updating your master list so that it is available for future adventures. In this way you can have a true master list for packing! Sample packing lists for various ages and adventures are included in the appendix for your reference.

The materials and gear that you carry with you for your babies will depend on where you are going and how you are getting there. If you are heading to a location with no baby gear available you will need to make some decisions based on how much you can bring with you and what money you might be willing to spend to rent what you think you need. Some hotels have cribs and pack-n-plays available for an extra charge. Some car rental companies also rent car seats. In larger cities and tourist destinations, baby gear rental companies can provide you with whatever you need and have it delivered right to your location- for a price. Be sure to look at cost differences between renting a stroller, for example, through a rental company for your entire trip and through a day location (where you will not have it available to take back to your car or use in the evening). When you have twins and are renting double, the fees can add up quickly. It is sometimes truly less expensive to purchase equipment at your destination then to rent it. Make sure to price out what you need in advance.

If you are visiting family and friends, be sure to ask them who they know who might be willing or able to loan you some baby gear. Even having only half of the equipment available at your destination can make things easier on you. On our first cross-country car trip we managed to pack two full-size high chairs (folded) and two pack-n-plays into our caravan, along with I'm sure a case of diapers and plenty of other baby gear! A subsequent trip, when we flew, did not allow us that flexibility. I was actually able to contact the local Parents of Multiples club at our destination and was able to borrow gear from a family who lived in that location. Parents of twins are a special set of people and are frequently willing to help out a fellow family with twins.

Travel by Car

There is no perfect way to travel- truly. There are, however, benefits to various modes of transportation and, because there is no perfect way to travel, you should definitely exploit those benefits! Car travel takes the prize for flexibility. There are no deadlines for getting on the road, no space constraints for overhead bins, and no paying by the piece of luggage- thank goodness! When you travel by car you can leave when you're ready, stuff gear into every square inch of space you can find, and pull off the road for a break whenever you need it. That being said, at times it can feel like you will never get where you are trying to go. It can be difficult to balance actually getting somewhere with the various needs the babies will want you to attend to which is difficult while all parties are buckled into appropriate seat belts. Your simple trips will double in length and your longer trips will feel like they take all day.

As with most other parenting tricks, travel by car gets easier with practice. You will figure out what to bring and where to pack it so you can reach it. You will figure out the best time to leave- when they are little, right before their longest nap is usually good, unless you have to stop to pay road tolls, in which case you'll want to sync-up nap time with uninterrupted road stretches! You'll want to figure out where the rest areas are and be sure to stop before everyone gets too hungry. You'll want to pack enough drinks and snacks for mom and dad- especially if you'll be nursing en route. Finally, as with all trips out of the home, you'll want to plan for three disasters and leave yourself enough time to get to your destination.

Travel by Plane

The benefits of traveling by plane are speed and freedom. For the most part, your "travel time" is limited. While the whole day is still easily devoted to travel, the amount of time you spend in the seat on the plane is likely limited to a few hours for a domestic flight. This minimal amount of travel time, per say, allows you (and hopefully a spouse) the freedom to attend to your babies as much as they need. Airports, while not entirely convenient, can be navigated with a plan and infant-care tasks can be completed with relative ease. Changing tables are available in the rest rooms, though honestly I found an empty corner to be far easier than dragging everything into a rest room. Waiting areas at empty gates can serve as staging grounds for nursing, walking laps with crying babies, or just generally staying out of the crowd while you wait for your flight to board.

Flying with twins requires slightly more legwork than traveling with a singleton. For purposes of this discussion, let's assume that two parents are flying with two children. Obviously your decision-making algorithm will be slightly different if you have other adults and/or children also traveling with you. First you must decide if your babies will be traveling on your laps or whether you will be buying one or more extra seats for them. Rules for infant and child travel should always be reviewed before decisions are made. Verify the rules based on the carrier you will be using, the age of the child, and whether the flight is domestic or international. Some parents buy a ticket for every passenger so that they can bring their babies' car seats onto the plane and their babies can be strapped into a seat they know and feel secure in. This allows the parents' arms a break and, it's possible, will help the babies to nap. Please note that you will want to verify that your car seat brand is certified for air travel to ensure that it will fit in the seat properly. This information should be available on the car seat itself, in the instruction manual, or on the manufacturer's website. Some parents choose to buy one extra seat- so that they have a place for one baby to be while the parents are able to pass the other back and forth. In many planes with rows of 3 seats this also allows the entire family to sit together. Both of these options are obviously dependent on the parents ability to purchase an optional ticket.

Many parents choose to travel with their babies on their laps. For budgetary reasons, this was the arrangement I always used when flying with my babies. I also generally felt like the babies would be happiest with mom and dad and certainly did not want to spend money on a seat we would not use! Generally speaking you will want to consider your babies' personalities- how much or little they want to be held on an average day, how easily they fall asleep, and how distressed they get in new environments. There is really no right answer- the decision is generally made based on whether the extra seat is affordable. Most important to note, however, is that seating arrangements with two lap babies must be discussed with the airline prior to the flight and, if possible, at the time of ticket purchase. Even if you purchase your tickets online and select your seat assignments at the time, you must contact the airline by phone to let them know you will have two lap babies. The airline will look up which exact plane will be used for your flight and will look at where the extra oxygen masks are for that plane. Only some rows have extra oxygen masks designed for lap babies and no bank of seats has more than one extra mask. What this means is that if two adults are flying with two lap babies, they cannot sit in the same bank of seats. Generally I recommend two aisle seats across from each other or in front and behind each other- depending on the layout of the airplane you are using. This will allow you to pass babies and supplies back and forth to each other and sit in different banks of seats. It is really important that you have this detail straightened out while there are still open seats to choose from. If you wait until the day of the flight, you will get moved and you will have to negotiate with others on your flight- you may end up a half a plane away from your spouse, which is not at all convenient for you or the babies!

Luggage

Decision-making when it comes to getting your family members and their gear onto the plane will vary greatly. Some families find it helpful to curb-check as much luggage and gear as possible, before they even park their car. These families will generally pull-up to the curb, unload all people and gear, check the luggage, and let one parent stay with the children inside the airport while the other parks the car in long-term parking- making sure to write down which lot and row the car is in before leaving. These families like the convenience of carrying as little as possible through the airport and trust the sky cabs to get their luggage to their plane.

Other families prefer to park offsite or carry all their gear inside to their air carrier or to the flight gate itself. If you choose this way you will need to give some thought as to how you will carry both babies and equipment through the airport. We found that we preferred to gate-check the most important gear- stroller and car seats- for fear of loss or damage. This also allowed us to have our stroller available for use throughout the airport and until the flight. To navigate the airport on one flight, we put the kids in front carriers (one on each of us), we put the car seats in the double stroller (because they were heavy), and we packed and hung carry-ons and diaper bags in, on, and around that stroller. We were a bit of a nightmare to get through security, but we made it!

The key to making a plan is to know exactly how many pieces of luggage you have, how many you are going to check, and at what point you are going to check them- curb, airline carrier line, or gate. Once you do this, you should think through who can carry what and what you will do if a baby doesn't like the method of carrying you have devised for them. With all of these decisions and plans, though, you are flexible and can attend to any baby's needs at any time- just be sure to build in enough time for three disasters!

Keeping Babies Happy

Successful waiting, both in the airport and in the air, is really no different than what you do at home. Try to anticipate what your babies will want at various times and be ready to meet those needs. I find travel to be the ideal time to attempt to keep as many people happy as much of the time as possible- mom and dad included! Get your coffee, give your solid food eating baby some favorite puffs or some tasty freeze-dried fruit pieces, pull out a new toy or book that you've been saving specifically for this trip. Books that have little sound buttons are especially enticing to the older baby and airplanes are loud enough, generally, that they will not disturb people in seats around you. I must admit, even if nearby passengers could hear the book sounds, I generally thought that they would prefer to hear organized book sounds than baby "scream and cry" sounds!

Some parents worry about the actual flight itself- the take-off and landing and how their babies will deal with the air-pressure changes. Some parents wonder about medicating their babies for their comfort, to help with ear pain or to make them sleepy. I advocate doing for babies what many adults do for themselves. Offer a bottle or snack or nurse your baby during take off or landing to encourage the baby to swallow and minimize difficulties with ear popping. Because air regulations and prohibited items are constantly changing, be sure to check with your airline about what is allowed to be carried on. If you are not able to pre-mix formula, ask a flight attendant for help filling your babies' empty sippy cups when you board the plan so that they will be full for take-off. Have plenty of individually packaged snacks so that should one bag end up all over the floor you have several back-ups. As hard as it may be to believe many babies actually do fall asleep when flying- perhaps due to the change in climate and perhaps due to a very simulating day before boarding! Once they are asleep, do everything in your power to keep them that way. I can still think back and remember just how asleep my arm was one trip when one of my babies fell asleep on it in just the right way! I've also never thought that the flight attendants spoke loudly- until I was worried they would wake my babies up!

The thing about travel is that I've found it always more difficult than anticipated- and I realize that's saying a lot. Being prepared, both mentally and physically, for some of the common issues is key. Sleep schedules and habits are almost certainly interrupted while you are away. Your day will look entirely different, and, therefore, your babies will not fall asleep when you think they should. Or, they will be tired from some activity and will sneak in an extra nap- making them less ready to sleep when you'd like them to later on. In the middle of the night they might wake up as they always do, except that the lights and sounds are unfamiliar and they will get upset and cry. Even if your baby is a wonderful sleeper at home, you cannot expect them to be that way while they are traveling. There is too much that is new and scary for them and they will seek your reassurance. Depending on the length of the trip they might even pick up a few bad habits and you will find yourself "sleep training" again when you return home. The good news is that once you sleep train your baby the first time, subsequent times are generally much faster and more effective.

For us, sleep set the stage for all other basic needs. When the babies were tired or sleeping on odd schedules they also ate at odd times and in various amounts. My children have always struggled to eat when they are tired. So, if you find that you are out late for dinner and your babies are not wanting to eat, try to adjust the times you feed them. Perhaps make sure they have a large breakfast or lunch and plan on them eating very little at dinner time. Try not to worry and not to force food at any particular time. The babies will be fine if they eat lighter for a few days and they will catch up and eat quite a bit when they are ready.

After a few too many trips where I was unprepared, I now count on someone getting sick while we are traveling. I always bring a "sick kid kit" which includes a thermometer, acetaminophen, and ibuprofen- along with little cups and syringes to dispense the medication. When the kids were little and we were still working out allergies I brought some Benadryl and Zyrtec as well! Make sure you have instructions from your babies' doctor about which drugs and doses are appropriate for your babies' weight and age. On our very first trip just a few hours away at Christmas, our daughter spiked a fever and, the truth is that it seems like we've had trouble with illness more frequently than reasonable while we've been traveling. Drug stores are not always convenient, or open, and who wants multiple thermometers! After a few run-ins with illness, we always pack our sick-kid-kit!

How to Have Fun

Having just read an entire chapter on how to navigate traveling, you might wonder what is the point. If life is hard enough at home, why, on earth would you increase the degree of difficulty! Because our family is out-of-state, we began traveling earlier, and travelled more frequently, than we likely would of normally. That being said, our mastery of travel also gave us confidence in our parenting skills and confidence in our preparations. We were comfortable taking our babies places- whether that was a mall an hour away for a day out or on a week-long trip a few states away.

The first step in enjoying your time is to feel that you are prepared for it. Use packing lists, ask questions of other twin parents, bring twice as much as you need- whatever will help you feel like you can handle whatever will come up. If your babies clothes are washed in special detergent, bring a little bottle in case you need to wash a few sets of clothes. If you're concerned about your baby's health needs, look up the contact information and address of a hospital or urgent care clinic near where you will be. Take whatever precautionary steps you wish prior to the trip so that when you are on it, you are not worried.

The second step to enjoying your trip is to keep your expectations low. When vacationing with your babies, your only goal should be to enjoy the time you have with them, wherever you are. If you are visiting a big city, then perhaps this will be your first time checking out all of the parks rather than the museums. Even if you are in a kid-centric location, perhaps your child is only old enough to sit up and splash in the zero-entry pool. Enjoying your time away from the routine and space of your everyday life and enjoying watching your children take in new experiences should be the goal of travel in the early years. Eat when you're hungry; get take-out and picnic on the lawn rather than worrying about your babies behaving in a restaurant. Spend more time enjoying them enjoying the day; spend less time figuring out what you should do.

Finally, I have found that time mellows my memories and that those "whitewashed" versions of events are actually very enjoyable. The hardness seems to melt away and the moments that I document in pictures become more salient. It is difficult, when your arms are generally full of babies, to take pictures and video. It is really important, though, to find a way to do something. Looking back at pictures, especially of trips and special events, help you remember all that you accomplished and all of the fun moments you had. I was never as good as I wanted to be about taking video, but I have thousands of still pictures from my babies lives. I have a hard time throwing any of them away- even the bad ones- as they all help me remember a moment. My son's facial expression makes me smile and my daughter's smile makes me grin. Documenting a trip through pictures, and especially how you, the parents, look at the time, is invaluable. Even if you hate getting your picture taken, make sure you get in a few.

Because, as a parent of twins, you spend so much of your lives in survival mode, the uniqueness of travel can offer you feelings of respite from the everyday. It is worth the time and effort to go places and try things. You will look back one day, not as far away from today as you might imagine, and realize the time you were enjoying was even more precious and short-lived than you expected. Seize the day.

23 JOURNAL: MAY 16TH

Tuesday, May 16th

Well, it was a year ago tomorrow that we found out we were expecting twins- my what a year it's been! We are both surviving and thriving- all at the same time. The babies are 8 months old by the calendar, and are approaching 7 months adjusted age.

They have developed a fondness for the messiness that is solid food, though Charlotte remains unimpressed at our attempts to get her to actually open her mouth for the spoon. Let me give you a play by play to illustrate the hilarity that ensues… it goes something like this:

Mom: "Would you like some squash, Owen?"

(Owen opens his mouth wide and takes a big bite. Mom shovels the food in as fast as she can, lest Owen begin to bang his hand on the highchair incase you didn't know he liked it.

Mom throws a spoonful into his mouth and sweeps up the excess that squeezes out his mouth and around his lips and chin, and throws that into the mouth in a second attempt.)

(While Owen is swallowing, mom looks to Charlotte)

Mom: "Charlotte, would you like some squash?"

(As mom begins to move spoon towards mouth, Charlotte looks on with interest but doesn't open her mouth.)

Mom: "Charlotte, open wide, go ummmm (mom opens mouth wide to demonstrate)"

(Charlotte remains unimpressed, but looks on with curiosity. Owen thinks this is the funniest thing in the world and opens his mouth wide to grin. All the previously shoveled food falls out.)

Needless to say, eating is an adventure. They very much enjoy drinking from mommy's glass, but still haven't figured out that there is water in the sippy cups (you know, the kind that doesn't get all over everything when they drink out of it). You can picture a similar scenario as described above as I try to demonstrate drinking from the sippy cup.

While eating and drinking continue to occupy a good portion of our day, we are tending towards some more predictable nap and play times. We're attempting (and for the most part getting) two naps every day. Much to mom's dismay, the naps have shortened to only about an hour each time. This, of course, is only enough time to shower and do one brief thing in the morning, and eat lunch and do one brief thing in the afternoon.

They are starting to really enjoy playing and are getting more curious and persistent in their adventures. Owen can really maneuver himself around if he wants to now. In fact, a pile of papers on the floor might as well be a neon sign for him. And if you relocate him to another area, hoping he forgot the previous goal, he will let you know that you were wrong. Charlotte still can't remember how to roll from front to back, and this can be problematic, considering her fondness for rolling back to front. But while she can't actually move, she is showing signs of wanting to pull up when she is next to something. Both are able to sit up unassisted for short periods-with Charlotte being more reliable at staying that way. They're having fun playing with their toys, and while I'm sick of them, they don't seem to be. We did recently have to go find a toy remote and a toy phone for them, as they felt that our versions were good toys. So far, they're content with our substitutions.

Well, we're working on getting packed up and ready to move-two weeks from today. I actually should be working on packing right now. This will probably be my last website update until we're in our new local… I must say, I'm so excited, but I may just miss this little apartment yet.

24 EATING SOLIDS

When to Begin

Generally people begin to give solid foods between four and six months. Figuring out what is right for your babies should be done with the guidance of their physician. We had to balance chronological age with adjusted age when making the decision for our babies. Our babies were six weeks premature; and my son had already experienced issues with an immature gut, like sensitivity to dairy (which I deleted from my own diet for the first 6 months I was nursing him). We chose, then to wait until they were at the late end of the guidelines according to their adjusted age. We started solid foods for our children when they were about seven months, adjusted (so, developmentally about 5.5 months). Along this same vane, we ultimately chose to consider adjusted age when beginning to offer cow's milk after the babies' first birthday.

We chose to make much of our own baby food as it was a budget friendly alternative to jarred food. Steamed and roasted vegetables are easily blended or pureed in a food processor with a bit of water. While more specific directions and recipes can be easily located on websites and in baby cookbooks, I found that I had the time and energy only for basic purees. I scooped these purees into ice cube trays to freeze the vegetables in approximately ounce-size portions. When the cubes were frozen I put all of them into labeled plastic freezer bags so that I could pull out portions as needed. To ensure that we had enough food out for each day, and to keep some kind of track over who ate how much, we used plastic containers- a specific kind that we didn't use for our adult leftovers, and color-coded for each baby. I would put the frozen cubes into the dishes each night and they would thaw in the refrigerator, ready by the next day when I wanted to use them. In this way I would also be able to keep relative track over how much each baby ate. Also, if one baby was especially hungry (or not) during one meal, I could easily save their leftovers for the next.

We did purchase organic cereal mix which we made with pumped breast milk as well as some pureed meats which were difficult to puree to the proper consistency with the blender we owned at the time. A few kinds of vegetables, even organic varieties, test high for certain chemicals. These types of vegetables (carrots were one for us at the time) should be purchased in jars, as ongoing manufacturer testing verifies food safety. Current food safety issues should always be researched, and verified online sources can be of particular help to new parents.

Feeding twins on a budget can require some "outside the box" thinking but is easy when you know what to think about. Purchase large jars of applesauce, rather than the baby food variety. Look at frozen adult vegetables that might already come pureed- in our grocery store winter squash was one of those varieties. Think about fruits and vegetables that are easily smashed- bananas and ripe avocado. The truth is that the "baby food" stage of life is short-lived and easily managed with a plan in place. Figure out what foods you want to introduce, on what schedule and in what order. There are a variety of opinions on what is best and I recommend consulting with your doctor about your babies' specific needs. Purchase and prepare foods a little bit at a time so that your freezer is stocked when you're ready.

Finger Foods

Your baby will quickly move from pureed to finger foods. The main concern with making this transition is managing your babies' risk of choking. Small bits of soft foods, like roasted sweet potatoes, bananas, and avocado are a good place to start. Some babies might have more trouble with swallowing than others. My babies took a while before they could manage larger bits of food. The Baby Puffs that are available literally melt in your babies mouthes and we ended up relying on those to make the transition to bigger bits of food. By the time my babies were one, however, they were eating all sorts of foods (despite a complete lack of teeth on one baby's part and barely any teeth on the other!). My babies loved the frozen mixed vegetable blends that contained things like carrots, peas, corn, and maybe green beans. It seemed to never fail that one baby would eat 2 colors and the other baby would eat the other two out of their bowls. It didn't take long before I just let them do that, then switched their bowls and watched as they ate what they wanted out of their sibling's dish!

Surviving Meal Time

The truth is that mealtimes can be somewhat stressful with twins. Generally both babies are hungry and want their food, immediately. This is not always possible if you need to assist with feedings, or if you are in the middle of another activity when the babies get hungry. As with everything twin, advance preparation is helpful if you can manage it. Make sure you have the bibs ready, drinks (if needed) prepared in advance in the refrigerator, and even dishes and silverware sitting out. Many parents of twins don't worry about sharing food, silverware, and cups between the babies. We are quite sure that they are sucking on each other's fingers and breathing on each other's faces the rest of the day, no need to worry about a few extra germs on a spoon. Do what is easy for you. For me, it meant a spoon in each babies' hand for banging and one spoon in my hand that alternated mouths!

Despite your best efforts, it is quite likely that food will be everywhere- on the floor, the high chair, and all over your babies by the end of the meal. In a classic story at our house, I was distracted (talking or doing some such thing) while I put tiny pieces of chicken on my babies high chair trays. As I realized a bit later, as I was putting one piece at a time on Charlotte's tray, she was putting one piece at a time on the floor.

If you plan for chaos and find that meals go better than expected you can give yourself a pat on the back. If you have high chairs with extra trays, remove the tray with the food prior to trying to wipe up your babies or you may find your efforts have been in vain. Finally, remember that the mess of food and babies is a staple memory of parenting and surrender yourself to the madness. The good news is, it's not time to start worrying about table manners yet!

25 JOURNAL: JUNE 26TH

Monday, June 26th

HAPPY SUMMER!

We are having a blast in our new house. We've made our way through the unpacking- not that everything is in its final place, but it is, for the most part, in a place. With the help of our families, the house and yard are put together and wonderfully livable. We've made our list of projects, as all homes have, and will get to them in time. We're loving the space (especially since we have no furniture!) and are enjoying the freedom of a single family home (hot showers on demand!). Some conveniences might never get old- our own washer/dryer, counter-space in the kitchen, and the attached garage are my current favorites!

Mike and I are trying to keep up with everything- house, yard, work, and babies, and so far, I think that we're realizing how much practice it could take to do it all well. The babies have adjusted relatively well to the move and are loving the house as well. I just reread my last babies' update and I can hardly believe how much progress they've made over the last month.

Over the past two weeks, Charlotte has taken the world by storm. She can now crawl, go from laying on her stomach to sitting, pull to her knees, pull to standing, is experimenting with balance (ie. Letting go of grip on things while on her knees or standing), and can pull herself up a step (though her size is the limiting factor there, she is just is not big enough to get up to the next stair). Along with all this momentous physical ability, she's developed an intense case of stranger/separation anxiety. This began about a week before we moved (which made the actual move and subsequent tasks a real challenge). She's pretty much a mama's girl right now. This was endearing for a day or two but mama would love to share the burden a little at this point. Charlotte, though, will have none of this.

Owen is a champion crawler, and can get across the room with massive strides if necessary (ie. If he locates something interesting that he knows we do not want him to get). He can also go from stomach to sitting, and can pull himself to his knees. Interestingly, he can reach the same things on his knees that Charlotte can on her feet, so he seems, thus far, to have no interest in going any higher. We now find them on their feet/knees in their cribs, talking to each other and laughing at the world at the end of their naps. Owen has been a gem with the move. He's been perfectly relaxed and happy to play with anyone who is interested.

We're working hard on finger food- and Cheerios have made their ever-important entrance into our babies' worlds. We're still working on getting the Cheerios into the right combination of fingers in order for them to be able to place them into their mouths. So, mom and dad have to sometimes offer some aid in order to temper frustration. The babies' continue to expand their diet and have been amazing at accepting new foods- they eat everything from avocados to apricots and beef to lentils! Hope that continues! Our new adventures are around slowly introducing textures (which so far they're not all that thrilled about). Cups (sippy and otherwise) continue to be a challenge they haven't mastered. We experiment with every combination of things- different cups, different combinations of valves (that let different amounts of liquid through them), etc. Both babies have been successful at getting some liquid from every combination of sources, just not consistently and not of any significant amount!

The babies definitely took some time to adjust to their new surroundings. Sleep patterns went haywire and for a day or two they were waking every two hours overnight again. Things started stretching out again finally, and for my birthday, the babies gave me the gift of a full night sleep (6pm-5am). This nicely coincided with our decision that they really were old enough and big enough to do it. So, once we got this good night sleep we decided not to turn back. The next two nights involved some unfortunate crying at 3am when they thought they should get a little snack, but, they did eventually fall back asleep. Then last night, mercifully, they slept all night (till 5am) without crying again. We can only hope that this is now the new normal. Interestingly, now that I'm getting a little more sleep, I'm actually feeling more fatigued- either that, or I'm awake enough to know I'm tired. The last 9.5 months are perhaps catching up with me.

Our days continue to be full with nap times, feedings, playtime, and attempts to offer new adventures to the babies. Yesterday we took our first trip to the swimming pool! The babies did great. Owen took a little time to warm up to the idea, but by the end realized that everyone was in one big bathtub and that water was fun. He loved bouncing up and down in the water with dad. He would get so excited that he'd slap his hands down onto the water and splash tons of water on his face. This confused him and it would take a minute to reorient. By that time, he'd be ready to do it again. Charlotte was enjoying gliding/walking through the water with mom and moving her hands through the water. Due to a poor afternoon nap, though, she was a little too tired to enjoy the trip to the fullest. Hopefully we'll get back to the water again soon.

So, our adventures continue. I think at this point no one expects any different, us included.

26 RELATIONSHIPS

There's not much that does not change when you have a baby. Most people know and accept that as a truth from the first moment they find out they are expecting. Having twin babies, I would argue, initiates those changes a little bit sooner and, overall, makes them that much more obvious. An area of change that is not discussed as frequently, however, is that of relationships. You have relationships with friends, family members and professionals that you interact with on a daily basis- one that is built upon the way you currently interact with the world. As your world changes, as the way you interact with the world changes, the way you view and interact with the people in it will change as well. Changing relationships is about more than just having less time for a girls-night out. It's about more than negotiating a more flexible work schedule for sick-baby days. Your relationships with those close to you and with those you socialize with will change because your way of interacting with the world is changing and you will need different things from those relationships.

From the moment my twin pregnancy was "diagnosed" my relationship with the medical community changed. My doctor changed as my care moved to the High-Risk Obstetrical Clinic. I became the patient of a team of doctors- in the OB clinic and in an ultrasound clinic I visited frequently to keep an eye on the growth of my babies. My relationship with my "baby turned babies" changed as I could no longer be sure of which baby was awake and which was kicking. When I was pregnant I tried desperately to hang on to the world as I knew it. I worked as hard as I could with my gradually fatiguing body to keep up my pace in my professional life. I tried to accomplish everything I previously did at home, despite my feeling constantly sick and more difficult to maneuver. I tried to keep my pregnancy issues only a topic of conversation rather than my whole world, so as not to annoy my non-pregnant friends. I tried to mitigate the changes in my life, so that they would not affect the rest of it, not admitting to even myself until later on that this was really impossible. No matter how you handle your changing world during pregnancy, those little blips in the road are nothing compared to the entirely different highway you will find yourself on when you return home with your babies.

MARRIAGE

I remember being in an undergraduate psychology class about Marriage and the Family. It was in a lecture hall full of a couple hundred people and the lights were dimmed so we could see the screen. A graph of "marital satisfaction" across the lifespan was being shown by use of an overhead projector- as some older professors still preferred and before powerpoint was ubiquitous. The graphed line was in the shape of a "U."

The short explanation was that everyone is happy at the beginning of their married life. As you become more accustomed to your new life and get into a routine, "satisfaction" begins to slip. Adding children significantly drops measures of satisfaction, and the early years with children are visually represented on the graph at the bottom of the U-shaped curve.

What you can learn and understand in a classroom always appears different in practicality. Having now had children, I understand much more intimately the changing moments on that graph. Having had twins, I have joked that we might need to modify the "normal" curve for parents with twins. Perhaps a "Q" would be more appropriate. With the precipitous fall timing up with an understanding of the reality of a twin pregnancy, down to the bottom of letter for endless nights without sleep, and reserving the "tail" (as I described it to my alphabet-interested children) for the toddler years filled with behavioral guidance and potty training times two. The fact is that anyone who is married will tell you that marriage takes work. And, anyone with kids will tell you that kids' needs can expand to fill all available (and less than available) time. How one learns to balance these seemingly conflicting, and both very important tasks, is challenging. "Tricky" as my children might say.

While every relationship will change, there is no more important relationship to navigate than that of your spouse and partner. It is in this relationship that you will most quickly see the changes and feel their impact. They are the ones who know how exhausted you are because they have watched you not sleep for days on end. They are the ones who help you through the daily drudgery and look at you with admiration for all you do. They are the ones who trudge off to work even when they cannot bare to leave their babies. They are your partner through it all. No one appreciates you more and no one makes you quite as upset when you feel as though they do not.

Relationship During Pregnancy

One of the relatively amusing things about pregnancy is how it can creep up on you. After feeling tired and run down for a week or two, suddenly, within an hour of a positive pregnancy test we had to pull over to the side of the road so that I could vomit. Any pregnancy, but especially a multiple-birth pregnancy, can take a toll on your body. I have friends with singletons who enjoyed a relatively uneventful pregnancy but I cannot say the same for my twin-mom friends. Speaking personally, I was sick- very, very, very, sick- for a good many weeks at the start of my pregnancy before the vomiting tapered down and I just managed with a low-level, twenty-four-hour-per-day nausea. My husband was supportive, when he was around. When we found out I was expecting he adjusted his work schedule in order to complete his hardest months of training before the babies arrived. He put in long days and many nights at the hospital, and I would try to find some humor in life while I was laying alone on the cold, blue, tile floor of the apartment bathroom, vomiting in the morning before dragging myself to work. Pregnancy symptoms seemed to come and go throughout the weeks and I generally say that there was only about a two-week window where I felt well enough to enjoy being pregnant. All of this, of course, was prior to my knowledge that there were, in fact, two babies!
With the realization of a twin-pregnancy, the medical community (including my husband) became watchful and

careful and the short-lived enjoyment of pregnancy evolved into more of a terror of what was to come. My own fear of the unknown, along with my husband's fear of everything that could go wrong (the downside of marriage to a doctor trained in obstetrics) led to caution in many areas. We did not take the trip I had hoped to enjoy as a two-some because it would take us away from the medical center. Marital intimacy suffered-both physically and emotionally as our time, attention, and stress was directed at keeping the babies from being born too soon. We felt that we had to be prepared for the babies to arrive far earlier than expected- both with simple things, like car seats, and with mental strength. Pregnancy was hard, our time together limited and practical. We started our careers as parents early and under stress.

How Things Change with Babies

My husband and I were married after he completed the third year of medical school- what might have been better labeled as the most challenging year of his education to date. We had been through more than a few difficult stretches of time during his schooling, where we had limited ability to see each other and even less time to enjoy pastimes or dates. The transition to parenthood was, for us, both a little bit familiar and a little bit sad. It was familiar in the sense that we had similar periods of strain before. We had gone through stretches where we didn't have enough time for each other- not just in the sense that we could not go out to dinner or sit and talk for hours about mundane topics like we used to, but in the sense that we did not even have a chance to communicate about our days or things that needed to happen for the household. If one has experienced this sort of "extreme living" you might understand what I am saying. If not, it probably is very hard to imagine how we literally might not have time to ask each other what time the meeting would be over the next night until it is, in fact, the next night and the person is on their way home from the meeting! The piece that was "sad" was that the time that we have spent in this state together has been longer than either of us anticipated.

While I may have expected our relationship to change with the birth of our children, I do not think I expected the extent of the change nor it's permanency. Not all change is bad, of course. I learned to rely on my husband in ways I never had to before. I trusted his plan and followed his lead at a time when I was both physically and emotionally compromised from the babies' birth. He knew what was important to me and he had our babies and my needs as his top priority. I can look back to those early days and know that he was taking care of me exactly how I needed him to. He did the small things, cleaning breast pump parts and pushing my wheelchair to the hospital Wendy's so that I could pick out my own lunch. And he did the bigger things- holding me when I cried leaving my babies at the hospital each night. When the babies came home he continued to help when he could, though he went back to work as his leave time had run out and was frequently only home for short periods of time. My most poignant memory of us as couple during those early months at home are of the two of us wearing matching baby carriers, each with a baby strapped to our chest, walking laps around the apartment, trying to get crying babies to sleep.

Our time together was functional- I often felt that we were like two employees, working on a project. For months we were sleeping in different rooms and neither our bodies or minds expected anything of each other. Fatigue was overpowering and the tasks of the day left little time or energy to spare. I remember our first trip out to dinner together, without the babies, after they were born. We went to a restaurant down the street and were gone for maybe an hour while family watched the babies. I remember thinking that it should have been fun- I had read the parenting magazine recommendations about getting out as a couple and about not talking about the babies. How you do that, though, when your life is enveloped by them, is something I never quite figured out. Over the years we've continued to go out to dinner on occasion, or have taken some time to shop for a few hours by ourselves. I don't know that I would ever really say that it "helped" me or allowed us enough of a break or rest to "reconnect."

As the babies grew we managed and our relationship matured. We improved our ability to enjoy each other while handling the functional tasks of parenting. We joked about our roles, calling my husband a "mule" as he was in charge of lugging all the gear we always needed and calling myself a "cow" as I was always nursing, or eating to produce more milk. We found humor when we could and our shared journey, impossible as it sometimes felt to describe to others, deepened our bond.

How We Handled It

Keeping your perspective while in the throws of twindom is challenging, at best. Fatigue drains one's patience and stress and strain is easily displaced, the spouse who has promised to stand by you through good times and bad becomes an easy target. You might begin to feel that if they would just do something different, help when you needed it, understand what you're going through, things might be more manageable. But the hard truth is this, it takes both of you, communicating, trying out roles and responsibilities to see what the best fit is for you as a couple. Everyone comes into parenting with a different set of expectations. Your family of origin, what you learned about being part of a family, is something you bring with you from childhood into your relationship. Spouses may not realize how different their expectations are from each other until they run into problems.

The first year(s) with children, and perhaps longer still, as you run into different developmental stages, will offer you a glimpse of how your spouse was raised. You will need to work as a couple to negotiate the differences and find a balance that is comfortable for you both. In our house a system developed where we try to honor the wishes of the "person who cares more." On any given issue one or the other of us might feel more strongly about what our family rules and expectations should be. When we don't have a strong opinion we try to give the other the final call. Because this is our expectation, it has been generally easy to compromise. No one ever feels like they are winning or losing on an issue, but instead we are taking turns with the final say. Generally speaking one or the other of us has had a stronger feeling about any given issue and, thus far, it's been a seamless way to structure our family.

There have been hard times and harder times, but we made a commitment to be here for each other and for our children. We both accepted that times were difficult and gave each other space as we tried to learn to be a wife and mother or a husband and father. We tried to adapt to each other's needs and played life a little bit by ear. As we now tell our growing children, things don't have to be "the same" to be "fair." In our house, fair means that each person gets what they need. Our needs are our own and we help each other by honoring them- whether that means that one person sleeps in every weekend day, or another gets some downtime for 10 minutes every night during the "bedtime routine." We are, in effect, trying to honor our marriage and the commitment we made to each other- by giving each other, individually, what we need.

Expectations

Everything I read while pregnant and all the people that I spoke with about life with twins kept referring to what almost became in my mind a magical time- when the babies reached a year. Everything, as I wanted to understand it, would get easier, go more smoothly, and be more clear to me if I could just get through "the first year with twins." What I would later learn is that there was nothing magical about that first birthday. I actually continued to find everything to be just as challenging, exhausting, and patience-trying as the day before. What I gradually came to understand is that what people might have meant is that "nothing gets worse." The fact is that life continues to change; it just gets different. The "survival mode" that we found ourselves in, probably beginning in pregnancy, continues through each successive stage and your goal should be to get a handle on managing it.

I purchased a book about Marriage and Twins at some point during my babies toddler years. I'm honestly not even sure what I thought our marital issues were at the time, or what kind of fix I thought I could find for them. I do remember reading the book, and then thinking at the end of it that it wasn't at all what I needed. There are varying degrees of marital strain and it is the level of distress that it causes between you and your spouse which should inform how it is handled. Some issues can be worked through with ongoing dialogue between partners and some is more appropriately addressed with the assistance of a professional. Understanding that stress and strain is a very normal part of adjusting to life with babies doesn't cure your relationship struggles, but it can make it seem slightly less dire. The ups and downs will continue as you hit developmentally challenging stages in your children's lives, and as you hit easier and harder points in your work or extended family life. Maintaining a joint commitment to working through difficult times, with each other or a marriage and family therapist, is the most important pact you can make with your spouse. Successfully navigating the rocky patches will make your marriage all the stronger and more fulfilling during the moments of calm.

FAMILY

Once you have children your role as a son or daughter quickly morphs into that of nanny and chauffeur- taking care of the grandchildren and getting them to the grandparents. Okay, well, not exactly, but your role as son or daughter can sometimes feel as if it has changed drastically when you have also become a mother or father. Second only to the excitement and anxiety felt by you and your spouse at the prospect of twins is that felt by your parents and in-laws. No other group of people will want as many details about how everyone is doing nor will think about you and the babies when they are not with you. They can provide invaluable levels of support and encouragement as well as tangible help when the babies arrive. Negotiating child-rearing differences between yourselves and your parents and in-laws can be tricky. Your history with each set of grandparents may inform your communication style and technique, but the truth is that there is no easy way around differences of opinion. As you become more experienced in your role, your views on parenting will change, as will your views on what parenting matters require consistency between parents and grandparents.

Your relationship with your extended family will be affected by how close you live to them and how alike your parenting styles are. If you live near your relatives and will see them on a regular basis, you will have to talk more frequently about more of the nuts and bolts of parenting- when and how much you want your baby fed, for example. If you see your relatives less frequently, you can learn to be more flexible with what happens when you're together. If you normally give your baby a bottle every 3 hours, and your relative thinks that your baby is hungry and wants to feed them again after two hours... well, that might not be an argument worth having on any particular day. It is important to remember, especially in the early weeks when you are so exhausted and your hormones are fluctuating most wildly, that everyone wants the best for your babies. What can seem like a really big deal can actually be ironed out fairly simply once you have identified what you want. You may wish to be the spokesperson for speaking with your family about issues and you may want your spouse to speak to theirs. Knowing the best way to talk to the parties involved can make hard conversations less difficult. Some issues- how you lay the baby down to sleep, or when to pick up a crying baby- have had different recommendations through the years. You should feel free to share what the current recommendations are and how you are handling them. You can also decide what to let go of from time to time.

Particularly with premie's, parents should feel free to blame the babies' doctors for any health-related decisions- the babies cannot be around second-hand smoke or strong perfume, people who are sick, people who have not had their pertussis booster, people who have not had their flu shot, etc. When my babies were born, we were advised to keep them away from as many people as possible for eight weeks after coming home. This was exceedingly difficult as so many of our friends and family wanted to come and hold the babies and visit with us. While we understood that it was really important to limit the exposure the babies had to germs during this time they weren't even supposed to be here, not everyone we knew felt the same way. When it comes to the health and safety of your baby, you must use whatever means necessary to enforce your family's needs and doctors are generally happy to be the scapegoat. These health matters can be particularly hard to negotiate with close family members, and they are often the first relational issues you have to manage as a new parent.

FRIENDSHIP

With two little beings taking over your day you will likely have little time for every other person you used to know! While you are acclimating to life with babies you will be lucky to think about calling anyone. I used to tell my friends to feel free to call me, that it wasn't that I didn't want to talk to them, it was just that I didn't think to call them! The difficulty that I had with friends when my babies were born is that I didn't feel like I was in the same place as any of them. My friends without kids were so carefree and their priorities were so different than mine now. I would watch my friends with singletons, even multiple singletons, have an entirely different parenting experience than I felt like I was having. I sometimes felt very alone in my world.

As a social worker I was familiar with the benefit of groups. A fellow social worker had given me information about the local Parents of Multiples group when I was pregnant. Looking back I have to chuckle about the fact that I didn't seek to connect with the group sooner. I honestly think I was in a bit of denial about the fact that I was having twins. I did get information from the group, however, when I was pregnant, and somehow they found me after the babies were born and some of the members brought me a few meals early on. A little bit of social connection- even just a quick smile as the meal was dropped off- and a fully prepared meal was a huge comfort at the time. I will never forget how I felt as I pulled a bottle of salad dressing out of the bag- they had thought of everything. I learned, at that moment, how it felt to be fully taken care of, and have tried to pay that favor forward.

Expanding your social circle to include families and friends with multiples specifically, will provide an enormous amount of support. Having fellow parents to call on a bad day or email for advice when one twin bites another will give you a really important outlet for your stress. There are some days that I was sure I wasn't going to get through, save for a fellow twin mom who sat on the phone with me for the last hour and a half of the day- she with her children and me with mine, both waiting for our working spouses to get home and offer parental back-up. These are the families who understand how many diapers one needs for an afternoon out, or how much work it is to meet you at the mall for the hour all four babies are awake but does it anyways because you need to get out. These are the families who understand why it isn't all fun and why you don't have cute pictures of yourself holding your babies the way other parents of singleton's do (there are two babies- no one has a free hand to take pictures).

For "stay at home moms" (SAHMs) it can be hard to get any, let alone "enough" social contact during the times your spouse is at work. It can frequently seem overwhelming to look ahead toward an entire day alone with the babies. The tasks of the day are many, downtime is likely non-existent, and it is very natural to feel alone in your world. My babies have always run on an early clock- their first nap of the day was frequently around 8:30am (before some kids were even waking up for the first time!). A fellow twin-mom friend had babies on a similar schedule and we were known to chat around 10am in the mornings, visiting while we fed babies their lunches! Creativity is key. Friendship is more than just going out to dinner. Friendship with twin babies means fulfilling your social needs in whatever way will work with your babies' schedules.

Working parents might struggle to expand their social group around their new parenting identify. Parents who miss their babies during the day while they work might not want to take time away from them when they are not working. If this applies to you, it is important, to continue your social relationships with your babies. Meeting up with other working parents and everyone's babies, at times convenient to work schedules, will offer you a social outlet while still allowing you precious time with your babies. Your connection with other parents struggling with managing work and home needs will likely leave you feeling refreshed and more confident as you continue your parenting and professional journey simultaneously.

27 JOURNAL: AUG 15TH

Tuesday, August 15th

Well, we crossed the 11 month mark last Friday, which means that we're less than a month away from the babies' first birthday. I seriously can't believe it. The heat of August has reminded me all too well of the agony of last summer, and yet, I sit here having a really hard time believing that my babies are now almost one!

"Everyone" has said that the first year is the hardest, and I've come to appreciate that statement in several ways. First of all, they've got to tell you something so that there's some glimmer of hope that this gets better. Second, I think it is the hardest cause you're not used to the level of chaos and constancy of movement and need. However, third, I don't think it gets better after the first year. The first year may be the hardest, which means nothing is harder- but I have a clear sense that it doesn't get any easier either. This has all become increasingly clear to me as the babies start to move, ever so much faster and in different directions, and think, about what they want to do, rather than what I want them to do.

We continue to have fun here- every day is an adventure and my fatigue is now a result of the speed of the day rather than the night wakings. There are some days (like yesterday) where I start counting the minutes till Mike gets home (you just hope the countdown doesn't start at 1pm), but other days the kids do well and you can actually clean up breakfast before you need to start dinner. The one challenging thing about having two babies at once is that unfortunately they can frequently cycle on opposite days, so your likelihood of having just a "good" day all around is really only 25%. Both can have good days, Charlotte can have a good day, Owen a bad day, Owen a good day, Charlotte a bad day, or both can have bad days- really only one of those scenarios is good for me!

Charlotte is crawling all over, and can turn on her jet propeller legs to get where she wants to go when she sees an open target (ie. Stairs, pantry door which contains trash can and fly swatter, door to mud room where interesting item is, as yet, unidentified, etc). She can pull to standing like a champ, has just in the past few days started to let go of things and can stand unassisted momentarily before dropping to the ground. She loves to pull up on the window sills and peek behind the shade in her room. She babbles when she's in a good mood, and most frequently at inanimate objects. She can make the mama and dada sounds, though we don't think she has a clue that they can be used as words, let alone words for us! She has learned to wave, though not on command- the action usually happens several minutes after our coaxing. She will, again, frequently wave at inanimate objects or other things that catch her interest (the wall hanging in her room, the television, the chandelier in her playroom, etc). Charlotte's two bottom teeth are in, and her two top teeth have just broken through the gums.

Owen is also crawling all over, he can pull to standing and has been experimenting with reaching over his head when he stands up. Just yesterday mom avoided a disaster when Owen figured out he could touch the top of the kitchen table, grab the edge of a placemat, and pull it, plate and all, towards the edge of the table. This reaching also applies to the cable box, television remotes, computer and associated cords and piano keyboard and associated cords. He's become quite a ham, and his big, wide mouth, toothless smile can light up a room. Owen has learned how to clap and is pleased to join in when everyone is having a good time. He also is becoming quite a chatterbox and frequently practices sounds for long periods of time. Sometimes he also adds a little body bouncing for rhythm. He has also said mama and dada, and we think might be starting to get that dada means something.

Dad is working on teaching both babies the appropriate hand gestures to go along with the phrase "Michigan touchdown" Luckily we've still got a couple weeks till football season starts.

Both Owen and Charlotte are doing well learning to feed themselves. We're trying to expand their repertoire of finger foods which is becoming more challenging as they seem to be becoming more picky about what they eat. Bananas, sweet potatoes, cheese, toast, and cheerios are the current favorites. They recognize the packaging of the Cheerios and YoBaby yogurt- both of which are serious favorites.

They continue to love stroller rides, books (and are starting to turn the pages themselves), and knocking down stacks of blocks. They've really started to play together a bit (for, like, 30 seconds at a time). But, it is very cute to watch them play peek-a-boo with each other as they chase each other around the couch.

Well, that's all the news with Charlotte and Owen! Mike officially started work on August 1st and he's enjoying all of the challenges that is bringing. I am formally resigning my position with the university to take care of the kids. We're continuing to love our home and have done a few minor modifications- essentially we've turned the dining room into a cute little playroom. It's in a perfect place right off the kitchen and down the hallway from the living room. It's a safe place where it's hard for them to get into trouble!

28 EMPLOYMENT

As your home life has changed dramatically, so too will your work life. No matter whether or when you return to your previous position, your view of the world at large has been forever changed. With a phone call that your babies needed you, you would walk out of the office. With a call that one was sick, you would no longer care about the meeting you were in. You have the poison control number and the doctor's office now programed into your cell phone. Whatever your intentions about work during your pregnancy and whatever plans you made for leave time and returning to work, there isn't much that you won't question when your babies finally arrive. Perhaps you planned to take a few months off before returning to work and after a few weeks you feel like you would be a better parent by getting back to work. Perhaps you planned to return to work in just 6 weeks because your employer has no ability to fill your position temporarily, and then your babies are born with medical needs. Perhaps you hope to take the time off your employer allows, and realize that child care for two infants costs more than your paycheck provides. There are not many clear-cut situations, and many parents are conflicted about their decisions, no matter how much choice they feel they have in the matter.

Making the Decision

While on the surface the decision about returning to work- full-time, part-time, or not at all- looks like a logical one, it is far more emotional. The cost of housing, cost of child care, and availability of health insurance are top factors for most families when considering how to best care for their bank account and children. An extremely important point to remember is that while this seems like a decision that is made and finalized, the truth is that no matter which direction you go, you will likely continually consider the others. If you look forward to returning to the job you love, you will still miss your children while away from them and wonder if you made the right decision returning to work. Further, if you decide to stay home and then don't find it quite as fulfilling as you had hoped, you may wonder why you gave up your professional life. The truth is that years down the road you might still find yourself evaluating the decisions you have made, wondering if they were, and still are, the right ones.

I enjoyed my work at a hospital prior to my children's birth and felt so fortunate that I was able to retain my status as an internal candidate for job applications for up to one year after my children's birth. My position was only held for a certain amount of time, and I knew prior to my babies birth that I would miss that deadline. Because the cost of two infants in daycare was higher than my salary (at least at the places I knew how to find at the time) we knew that it did not make financial sense to go back to work right away that first year. I was aware that the babies would likely be premature and, as babies born in the fall season, I was worried about them picking up germs and illness over the winter in a day care situation. I can honestly say that I did not have plans to go back, or not to go back, to work when the babies were first born.

Having twins did play a significant role in my work versus stay-at-home-mom (SAHM) decision-making. Had I had one baby, and the cost of day care potentially not taking my entire salary, I'm not entirely sure what I would have done. I do know that having two babies (premature, twice the child care cost, twice the germ exposure in day care, and twice the potential missed days at work due to babies getting sick) was the primary factor in my decision to stay home initially. Furthermore, my husband was in his last year of his medical residency program at the time and his schedule was not at all flexible. The primary responsibility for juggling babies' needs fell to me- and I was glad to do it. At some point over that first year, I realized that I was in the right place at that point in my life. We were making ends meet on his residency salary and felt fortunate to be able to structure our life in a way where that could continue. The flexibility that I would need in a job, as well as a salary that would at least cover the babies' child care costs, were the most important considerations for us. At that time, a job with the right equation of hours, money, and flexibility did not outweigh what I was worried about missing and what I felt like my babies could use from me. My staying home was the right thing for us at the time.

Feeling Okay with the Decision

A former supervisor told me many years ago that she and her husband had decided, when it came to parenting issues, that they could do anything for six weeks. They decided that six weeks was long enough to give them time to adjust and work out the problems, but short enough so that they felt like they could tolerate the situation if it just didn't work. I have thought of that piece of advice periodically, as it applies to so many areas of life and makes all decisions seem that much less permanent. Try something for six weeks, then give yourself permission to change. If you go back to work after your babies are born, give it six weeks for everyone to adjust. If it's not working after that, try something different. Figure out what is and is not working and try slight adjustments to see if the new situation is tolerable. Likewise, if you don't think you want to return to work and feel as though you must, give it six weeks of being home with the babies and then try to ease back into work- perhaps you'll find yourself renewed when you return home to see the babies.

I am quite convinced, after spending many years as a SAHM, that there is no "right" way to be a parent. There is nothing better about a parent who works or one who stays at home. All roles require management, patience, and flexibility. In the same way, all roles can become tedious, burdensome, and depressing. Whether it is the mother, the father, or another loving caregiver with your child during the day or night, your children will know the role you play in their life. They will seek you out to meet their needs, whenever you are with them. They will miss you when you are gone- whether that is for a trip to the bathroom or a trip across country for your job. Saying goodbye to them, for an hour, a day, or a week will take practice, and it will get easier, for them and for you. Keeping your spirits up, regardless of what role you play each day, is an essential part of being successful in your work- both in home and out.

Professional Mom

My experience has been that of a professional turned SAHM. While I'm quite sure that each individual's path through parenting is unique, I would argue that there are some common themes worth noting. As with any new position one takes outside of the home, finding your professional identity in your role as mom will take time. When you are used to feeling competent at work, it can be slightly unnerving to to find that such a few small pounds of baby can make you feel completely inept! If you are used to making decisions, putting together plans, and overseeing work get accomplished, you might find yourself in shock as you see how very little might "get done" all day at your home. When the goals of your day change from managing very serious issues to counting wet diapers and minutes of nursing, you might find yourself both confused and uncertain about what and how you are doing.

With each day that passes and each successful exchange with your babies, your confidence in your role as mom will grow. Being a SAHM will mean different things to different mothers and you will need to learn to define your own goals and meet them on your own terms. Being home with your babies does not mean you will necessarily have a clean house or make gourmet meals. Being home with your babies might mean that you are on the go- taking them to play groups, attending parenting support meetings, and stimulating their minds out in the world. Some mothers will thrive with the adventure of unplanned days and the opportunities that await their children. Other mothers will struggle to enjoy outings and events structured around naps, feeding, and family schedules. Finding out who you are, as a mother, takes time and experimentation. If you enjoy that challenge you might enjoy being home with your kids.

Adjusting to life at home can be challenging, though, in ways you might not expect. The larger society frequently has opinions about SAHMs, whether based in reality or not. You might find yourself with less to talk about in adult settings, you might find that others don't really know what to ask you about- not having a career to inquire about. You might find that schools, groups, and the community look to you to volunteer your time and skills because they do not see you as busy with other things. Stay-at-home-dads must contend with all of the above-mentioned challenges and at the same time fight cultural, and perhaps family, stereotypes as well. SAHDs are certainly outnumbered in playgroups and at story times, and, yet, they need the same reinforcement and social connection that the moms do.

As with parents who return to work outside the home, staying at home permanently will take time to adjust to as well. You may find yourself continuing to adjust your expectations of yourself, or you may find yourself struggling to keep those expectations realistic. We can only ask ourselves to do our best, not to be perfect.

Returning to Work

Parents of multiples will find themselves returning to work at some point. Whether or not you are leaving your babies with your spouse or another loving caregiver, you will likely have mixed feelings. Perhaps you are looking forward to a break from the constant demands of feeding, changing, and getting babies to sleep. Perhaps you feel guilty about leaving a spouse or caregiver to play zone defense. Your job is important to the functioning of the family too. Your income is providing for food, shelter, and clothing- essential needs of your new babies. Likening your family to a team and remembering that on a team players play different positions can help you reframe your return to work. You are doing your part for the family and that is important too. Overtime time you will find your groove- perhaps you can enjoy smiles with the babies before you leave in the morning, or perhaps you like to take the babies for a ride in the stroller when you get the mail in the evening. Perhaps you have the magic to give the babies a bath without crying or know just the song that puts them to sleep each night. It is not the amount of time you spend with them, but how you spend the time you have that is the most important. Focus on what you add to their lives and not on the hours you are not with them.

You may find that having periods away from the demands of your babies will mean that you must work even harder at coping with their changing needs while you are with them. As a SAHM mother myself, I used to notice that some tasks were more difficult for my husband as he had less time to practice and it was not always as obvious to him that the babies had matured and could handle a different responses to a situation. When there are gaps in the time you spend with your babies it can be more challenging to adjust to their changing needs. You must have patience with yourself and watch other caregivers for clues about these changing needs and reactions. Babies can change by the hour and you must let go of any guilt you might have about not being there for the transition. Keeping up with babies is a full-time job in itself.

Remember that everyone has their role to play and that not everyone needs to be an expert on each task.

Changing Your Mind

Remembering that the work-life balance is forever on a scale, and can always be changed, is an important part of making any work plan succeed. There is no right, there is no wrong. Some decisions might be harder at certain points in your life, or in the life of your babies, but the truth is that those hard moments might have to happen sometime, and it is possible that the hardness will be there waiting in the future. Some parents have to return to work just six weeks after their babies are born, and will likely struggle when that transition comes. For SAHMs, though, perhaps they take their children's transition to school a few years later harder than working parents who have already learned to say goodbye. If you remain home with your children throughout their school years, you may find college to be the most difficult transition as your babies leave home for good. As my husband reminded me early on, the goal of parenting is to to make yourself obsolete. Part of learning to be a parent is learning how to be okay with doing that. I don't happen to think it gets easier, no matter when it begins.

29 JOURNAL: SEPT 11TH, 27TH

Monday, September 11th

A Year in Review…

To celebrate the babies' first birthday, the pictures in the website photo gallery include some of our very favorite memories from the past year. We have not posted all of the cutest pictures, but instead, the ones that capture the moments that we remember most fondly.

Watch us grow! There is at least one picture from every month, and pictures are in chronological order.

It's been an incredible journey so far.

Happy 1st Birthday to Owen and Charlotte!

Wednesday, September 27th

Happy September Everyone!

Things here are going well. The kids are doing great- becoming ever more curious, mischievous, and charming by the day. We've now celebrated their first birthday, and, just this past Sunday, the anniversary of their homecoming. As it has now been over 365 days that I have been on-call 24/7, I've asked Mike for a vacation. I've been granted one on September 15th, two years from now! Little does he know I'm going to hold him to it.

Charlotte marked the anniversary of her homecoming by taking her very first steps- 3 of them- to reach the slide that she was given for her birthday. (As I understand it, my sister, her aunt, took her first steps to get to her slide when she was little.) Mom was present for the occasion, and dad was quickly called into the room. Luckily Charlotte was willing to do two encore performances so that mom and dad could really believe their eyes. Charlotte is becoming ever more mobile by the day, though she seems to prefer to practice her vertical motion- she's very much enjoying climbing up and down the slide, and has begun crawling up as many of her other toys and furniture as possible. It's particularly heart-stopping to watch her climb up to the top of her walking toys, which are, of course, on 4 wheels. We've got quite an acrobat on our hands!

Owen is doing wonderfully as well and is channeling his attention to some gross motor tasks. He very much enjoys pushing things around the room- his trucks, his cups, cans of Coke that he and Charlotte unpack from the cabinet... He loves to practice taking blocks off of the top of towers that we build- without knocking down the whole tower. So far he generally takes off two blocks (one for each hand) before getting so excited that he knocks over the rest of the tower.

Both babies are becoming quite the babblers and we're certain they're fluent in several different languages. They've both found some favorite sounds that seem to be the answers to some of life's toughest questions. I don't really know how to "spell" sounds (some of you might reference my spelling of all things, but we'll leave that one alone for now), but for the sake of posterity, I'll try. They're both quite fluent in mama and dada and will use them interchangeably and to signify any and all needs and wants. I'm looking forward to the day when those sounds become nouns, and not imperative statements! Charlotte likes to say "beez beez" and "gaw gaw" sometime throwing a "ba-gaw ba-gaw" in there. Owen uses "doh, doh" and "ta ta." Both of them will use their sounds of choice quietly, loudly, in melody, or as commands- as the situation requires.

They're doing great eating and growing, though are still helping to define the lower edge of the growth curve. They're eating table food and have started drinking whole milk. They're still not crazy about the sippy cup, though this is one issue I will be forcing for convenience! They do mediocre at getting in the fluids each day, but I am certain that with patience (that's much easier found at 9pm after they've been sleeping for 2 hours) we will prevail! I hope to be weaning them completely in the coming weeks.

Mom and dad are doing well, attempting to find a new rhythm

in life which incorporates all of our necessary tasks and chores, ongoing activities and hobbies, and any unique opportunities that present themselves. With little to no time in the day to devote to any of these three areas, this has been quite a challenge.

But, our adventures continue here as always, and I very much enjoy sharing them with all of you. Hope you're having a wonderful fall and we love to hear from you, also, as you have a chance.

Love,
Elise, Mike, Charlotte, and Owen

30 MEMORIES

Each day can feel like an eternity, but the years move quickly and your babies will grow right before your very eyes. Newborn sleepers will get too tight and pack-n-plays that once held both babies width-wise will suddenly be filled up by one stretched out baby. Your tiny little balls of baby will turn into responsive, smile-filled, rays of sunshine. Jobs that used to be tricky, like diaper changes on barely moving newborns you will now be able to complete one-handed while pulling the next baby over for their turn. Your competence will soar and the love you have for your babies with it. Your role as a parent will become more defined and you'll feel more comfortable with what jobs, activities, and obligations allow you to fully embrace that role. Before you know it you will become the person getting calls from new parents of twins, and you'll know just what to say to them to help them through the moment and assure them that they are in it for the long haul.

Whether your twins are your first, your last, part of your many, or your only, the days with them move quickly and the moments you might imagine you will have, of quiet contentment and reflection, can be few. Raising twins is an experience unlike any other. The demands for your services- both physical and emotional- are never-ending and finding the energy and strength to meet those needs can be exhausting. But amidst all of the hard, and all of the fatigue, there are moments of pure joy- for you and for your babies. Learning to focus on those moments and burning them into your memory (or at least writing them down so that you someday remember they happened) can help you not just get through the difficult days, but can help you enjoy your parenting experience.

How to Remember

Ways of sharing stories, remembering moments, and documenting events continue to evolve rapidly. New electronics and new programs continue to emerge and allow parents ways of taking pictures, taking videos, and recording stories. Even with the best of intentions, it can be tricky to keep up with any one form of recording, let alone all of these.

When my babies were born we had a camera, we had a video camera, and we had a website (which seems like an ancient relic compared to what is available now). Our families lived out-of-state and we knew that we wanted a way to share our babies' story with them. I set up the website when I was pregnant- sharing stories and pictures before they were even born so that I could learn the program and know what I was doing when they arrived. We did a decent job taking pictures and recording some little moments on the video setting on our camera that first year. (Note for the future: It is far easier to take those pictures during the first year when they're not really moving- it gets a LOT harder later on!) We very much appreciated when family came to visit and took pictures that they shared with us. We did not do very well taking actual video, and despite my best efforts to be deliberate about it over the years, I have never really been able to make it a routine. I did a fairly good job updating the website over the first year, though reading back I see how much I didn't say about our days and life. I enjoyed the writing, though, and found the reading back of it to be enjoyable. As the years have gone on, I have expanded both my documentation and detail. My children will have a very complete record of their childhood someday!

Knowing what you enjoy doing and looking at is important. The fact is, that with two babies and two parents there really isn't anyone else left to hold the camera on an average day- the same reason that it is commonly joked about that second children don't have as many pictures as the first child does. With one baby and two doting parents there is always someone to take a picture. For me, I knew I loved to look at still photographs and that was my primary way of recording the babies that first year. While I didn't take much video, the truth is that I don't go back and watch the videos I did take very often either. It is just not my way of connecting to the memories. My enjoyment of journaling, and later blogging, has evolved over my children's lives. While the first year is less descriptive than later years, it allows me glimpses into their lives that I would have otherwise forgotten. Which sounds each baby made, for example, are little bits of memory that I'm sure I would have lost had they not been written down. For my baby shower, my sister gave me a decorated can with little papers and a pen. I was supposed to write down little notes, with the date, like "baby's first tooth" and then drop them in the can. It seemed so easy to do, and yet, I was never able to make it happen. The truth is that I really have no record of when each of my babies got their first tooth! However you choose to record their lives you must pick something realistic. If you find that whatever you choose is not working in the first few months, assume it won't work in the future and try something else new. I found that despite my best intentions, if it wasn't something natural for me, I couldn't make it happen.

How to Share

For many people, the whole point of recording the pictures and memories is to share them. Today's electronic gadgets and programs allow parents to take photos, videos, and notes all on one device and share it with the world instantly. Some parents find this liberating and others are more cautious. Without addressing the pros and cons of any specific device or program, here are some things to keep in mind when sharing your news and memories with others.

Backing-Up:

Unfortunately I know far too many people who have lost their pictures, documents, and videos to an untimely electronic malfunction. Whether you store your pictures on computer hard drives (internal or external), in print, on flash drives, DVDs, or in "the cloud" make sure you have multiple back-ups available. Devices get damaged, discs give out, files "disappear." These are some of your most precious memories and deserve to be backed up, lots of times. We have our pictures on an internal hard drive and back up our computers to an external hard drive. After a brush with natural disaster we now store our external hard drive in a weather and fire proof safe. I try to back up my online blog posts into a standard word processing document stored on my computer (which is backed up to the external drive).

Privacy:

When your baby is little they don't know what you are sharing about them, nor will they eventually probably care when they are older. At some point, though, they will be older enough that they will understand that you are talking about, writing about, and sharing their news. Always keep in mind who your audience is and whether you would want the information you are sharing public forever. In my writing, I have always tried to write after the raw emotion has dissipated. If I'm upset or happy or mad I try to wait and write later on when I have cooled off a bit. I once wrote that I liked the "selective remembering" of blogs. The moments are whitewashed a bit- both for public consumption and with the general mellowing of my temper with the quiet of sleeping children.

Further, sharing information and pictures digitally leaves that information open to the world. Some parents like to watermark their pictures so that they can't be used elsewhere and claimed as something they are not. Some share pictures of their kids only with their close friends or prefer that they not be online at all. In an age when information technology is rapidly expanding, at a rate where we don't even know what and how that information can be used, it is wise to be thoughtful about where and what information is available to the public about your children.

Retrieval:

Posting notes over the days to social media can be fun, but make sure you have a way to sort, organize, and save those posts for the future. If you send a nice letter or email to a family member about your babies, make a copy or flag the note in your email so that you can save the memories for yourself as well. Each post or note, in itself, doesn't seem like a big deal, but over the years, which pass far faster than you might imagine, you have written a story without even knowing it. No matter how you choose to share your news, make sure you know how to consolidate your notes for the future. At the very least, copy and paste each note into a dated word-processing document.

When You Don't Want to Share:

Not everyone wants to share information about their babies over the internet and some live with all of their family close by and share in person. Some don't want to share their writing and others don't want to share their struggles. Remember that the memories you save are for you and they are for your children. Keeping them does not mean you need to share them. Remembering the days you have successfully mastered will help you get through future days of hard. Some people like baby books where the questions are already written and only require that you fill in information. Others prefer to keep a private journal, either hand-written or in their own word-processing document designed only for personal use. However you choose to save your memories, choose what is comfortable so that you will enjoy and continue doing it.

What has survived over the years? I still use my camera (and have upgraded to a nicer one). We still have our video camera, and use it to record certain events- like Christmas morning and dance recitals. I have a Flip video camera which was supposed to help me catch smaller recordable moments now that my fancy camera does not take video. I must admit to only using it occasionally. And, I blog, on a password protected site, available to family and friends that I have invited to keep up with us. Blogging allows me to remember the good and fun moments of life in spite of the hardness of much of parenting and adulthood in general. It gives me a space to write down the one-liners and silly stories and functions like a yearbook of sorts.

There is no "best way" to save and collect your pictures and videos. I must admit to being drastically behind on printing pictures of any form- either prints for frames or making photo books. My children love to look at the pictures, though, and what I do have they often enjoy. You can make books by event or by year, by child or by activity. There are almost too many choices for parents of twins! Thus far our family has found chronological family albums to be the most enjoyable, as generally the pictures include many of us and we can enjoy looking back at the events of the year. Digital pictures have allowed us the flexibility of grouping pictures in many ways and perhaps someday I will go back and make a book of highlights of each child individually. Right now, though, our story is together and that works for us.

What the pictures, video, and writing do, in all instances, is help us focus on and remember the moments throughout the days and weeks which are most enjoyable, most unique, and memory-worthy. You will remember the time both babies were undressed for bath and you were caught off-guard with no one diapered and everyone needing one. You will remember nursing, overall, and perhaps moments, like the first time they held each others' hand while doing it. You will remember the 4am feedings and the 4pm melt-downs. Through pictures you will remember how cute your babies were when they somehow wiggled right next to each other and you will remember how young you looked when it all started.

Take pictures of your babies, have others take pictures of you. Don't be bashful, be sure that you will someday want to see how tired you looked, or how content your daughter was in your arms. Take that 30 seconds to scribble down when that first tooth came in, someday you will wish you did (trust me!). Having twins is an adventure, an adventure worth retelling. Stories, photos, and videos help with that retelling and will make you smile for all the years to come.

APPENDIX I:
DIAPER BAG SUPPLIES

Keep Packed at all times:

- Diapers for each baby
- Wipes
- Changing pad
- Extra change of clothes for each baby
- Burp Cloths
- Snacks (for parents and babies)
- Plastic baby silverware (for when you find yourself unexpectedly out to eat)
- Bottle/Formula Supplies
- Plastic Bags for dirty diapers (look for little rolled packs sold in baby supply aisles)
- Hand sanitizer
- Notepad and pen (for everything you might need to remember)

Add each trip out:

- Wallet
- Keys
- Phone
- Prepared bottles

APPENDIX II:
EMERGENCY ROOM PACKING LIST

- Cell Phone & Charger
- Keys
- Wallet & Cash
- Diaper Bag(s)
- Breast Pump
- Personal Supplies: comfortable clothes, slip-on shoes, toothbrush, toothpaste, hairbrush, hair ties, glasses/ contact solution, book, electronic device/computer and charger.

APPENDIX III:
SAMPLE PACKING LIST FOR TRAVEL

Equipment

White Noise Machine
Baby Monitor
Pack & Play (2) & Sheets
Stroller
Baby Bjorn (2)
Diaper Bag (2)
Blankets
   Floor/Changing
   Sleeping/Cuddling
   Going out

Supplies

Diapers/ Swim Diapers
Wipes
Diaper Rash Cream
Lotion
Nail Clippers
Hairbrush/Comb
Bath Wash
Burp Clothes
Waterproof Pads
Tylenol/ Thermometer
Pump/ Pump Supplies
Travel Highchairs
Sunscreen
Bug Spray

Clothes

Onesies
Sleepers
Outfits
Socks/ Tights
Shoes
Hats
Coats
SwimSuits

Toys

Train
Ball
Drum
Links
Teethers
Blanket Toys
Books

Food

Bibs
Bowls
Spoons
Sippy Cups
Wash Clothes
Food/ Cereal
Finger Foods

ABOUT THE AUTHOR

Elise Moultrup Bruderly has a Bachelors in Psychology and a Masters in Social Work from the University of Michigan in Ann Arbor, Michigan. Her lifelong interest in the human condition and psyche has been focused on parenting issues over the last nine years as a result of her personal experience becoming a parent of twins. Holding positions of Chair, Board member, and group member in her local Parents of Multiples group over the past eight years, she has been an active participant and contributor, assisting fellow parents through difficult stages and times. The author enjoys synthesizing general singleton-parenting advice and research-based parenting literature and adapting the information for use in families with multiples.

Prior to expanding her career into parenting, Elise Moultrup Bruderly worked as a Clinical Social Worker at the University of Michigan Hospitals and Health System.

Made in the USA
San Bernardino, CA
02 April 2016